EMOTIONAL AND MENTAL HEALTH

MACMILLAN
HEALTH
ENCYCLOPEDIA

5

50.00

EMOTIONAL AND MENTAL HEALTH

MACMILLAN LIBRARY REFERENCE USA
Simon & Schuster Macmillan
~~NEW YOR~~K

Simon & Schuster and Prentice Hall International
LONDON • MEXICO CITY • NEW DELHI • SINGAPORE • SYDNEY • TORONTO

MACMILLAN
HEALTH
ENCYCLOPEDIA

5

EDITORIAL CREDITS

Developed and produced by
Visual Education Corporation, Princeton, NJ

Project Editor: Darryl Kestler

Editors: Richard Bohlander, Susan Garver, Michael Gee, Emilie McCardell, Cynthia Mooney, Suzanne Murdico, Frances Wiser

Editorial Assistant: Carol Ciaston

Photo Editors: Maryellen Costa, Michael Gee

Photo Research: Cynthia Cappa, Sara Matthews

Production Supervisor: Anita Crandall

Proofreading Management: Amy Davis

Art Editors: Maureen Pancza, Mary Lyn Sodano

Advisor, Anatomical Illustrations:
David Seiden, Ph.D.
Robert Wood Johnson Medical School
Piscataway, New Jersey

Layout: Maxson Crandall, Lisa Evans

Word Processing: Cynthia Feldner

Design: Hespenheide Design

The information contained in the *Macmillan Health Encyclopedia* is not intended to take the place of the care and advice of a physician or health-care professional. Readers should obtain professional advice in making health-care decisions.

PHOTO CREDITS

Jacket: Howard Sochurek/The Stock Market

The Bettmann Archive: 71

H. Armstrong Roberts, Inc.: Jansen, 93

Neal and Molly Jansen: 67

John Fitzgerald Kennedy Library: 55

Leo de Wys Inc.: Ann Chwatsky, 75; Rocky Weldon, 46

Richard B. Levine: 74

Sara Matthews: 26, 31, 64 (bottom)

Mary Messenger: 57 (left)

Midwestock: Wally Emerson, 76

Cliff Moore: 41, 51 (bottom)

The Norwegian Information Service in the United States: 11

PhotoEdit: 72; Bill Aron, 59 (top); Bill Bachman, 45; Robert Brenner, 6 (top), 19 (right), 23 (middle), 35 (top), 84 (bottom); Jose Carrillo, 64 (top); David Conklin, 37; Mary Kate Denny, 28, 33, 80, 100, 101; Amy Etra, 19 (left); Myrleen Ferguson, 48, 50, 54, 59 (bottom), 89, 95; Tony Freeman, 5, 14, 30 (bottom), 47, 69 (left), 69 (right), 84 (top), 85, 92, 98; Freeman/Grishaber, 7; Wendy Malecki, 35 (bottom); Felicia Martinez, 23 (right); Stephen McBrady, 23 (left), 58; Sebastian Papenberg, 91; Vicki Silbert, 57 (right); David Young-Wolff, 52, 82, 90, 97 (right)

Photo Options: Ed Malles, 32

Rainbow: Dan McCoy, 18, 97 (left); Hank Morgan, 27, 51 (top)

Frances M. Roberts: 68, 73

Terry Wild Studio: 8; Geisinger-Marworth, 49

Unicorn Stock Photos: Robert W. Ginn, 30 (top); A. Gurmankin, 17; Martin R. Jones, 6 (bottom), 53; MacDonald, 40

Zephyr Pictures: Melanie Carr, 12

From WHEN RABBIT HOWLS by The Troops for Truddi Chase. Copyright © 1987 by Truddi Chase. Introduction and Epilogue Copyright © 1987 by Robert A. Phillips, Jr., Ph.D. Used by permission of the publisher, Dutton, an imprint of New American Library, a division of Penguin Books USA Inc., and also by Sidgwick & Jackson: 64 (bottom).

SIMON & SCHUSTER MACMILLAN
Macmillan Library Reference
1633 Broadway
New York, NY 10019-6785

Printed in the United States of America

printing number
10 9 8 7 6 5 4 3

Library of Congress Cataloging-in-Publication Data

Macmillan health encyclopedia.
v. <1- >
Includes index.
Contents: v. 1. Body systems—v. 2. Communicable diseases—v. 3. Noncommunicable diseases and disorders—v. 4 Nutrition and fitness—v. 5. Emotional and mental health—v. 6. Sexuality and reproduction—v. 7. Drugs, alcohol, and tobacco—v. 8. Safety and environmental health—v. 9. Health-care systems/cumulative index
ISBN 0-02-897439-5 (set).—ISBN 0-02-897431-X (v. 1).—ISBN 0-02-897432-8 (v. 2).
1. Health—Encyclopedias. I. Macmillan Publishing Company.
RA776.M174 1993
610′.3—dc20 92-28939
CIP

Volumes of the *Macmillan Health Encyclopedia*

1 *Body Systems* (ISBN 0-02-897431-X)
2 *Communicable Diseases* (ISBN 0-02-897432-8)
3 *Noncommunicable Diseases and Disorders* (ISBN 0-02-897433-6)
4 *Nutrition and Fitness* (ISBN 0-02-897434-4)
5 *Emotional and Mental Health* (ISBN 0-02-897435-2)
6 *Sexuality and Reproduction* (ISBN 0-02-897436-0)
7 *Drugs, Alcohol, and Tobacco* (ISBN 0-02-897437-9)
8 *Safety and Environmental Health* (ISBN 0-02-897438-7)
9 *Health-Care Systems/Cumulative Index* (ISBN 0-02-897453-0)

PREFACE

The *Macmillan Health Encyclopedia* is a nine-volume set that explains how the body works; describes the causes and treatment of hundreds of diseases and disorders; provides information on diet and exercise for a healthy lifestyle; discusses key issues in emotional, mental, and sexual health; covers problems relating to the use and abuse of legal and illegal drugs; outlines first-aid procedures; and provides up-to-date information on current health issues.

Written with the support of a distinguished panel of editorial advisors, the encyclopedia puts considerable emphasis on the idea of wellness. It discusses measures an individual can take to prevent illness and provides information about healthy lifestyle choices.

The *Macmillan Health Encyclopedia* is organized topically. Each of the nine volumes relates to an area covered in the school health curriculum. The encyclopedia also supplements course work in biology, psychology, home economics, and physical education. The volumes are organized as follows: 1. *Body Systems: Anatomy and Physiology;* 2. *Communicable Diseases: Symptoms, Diagnosis, Treatment;* 3. *Noncommunicable Diseases and Disorders: Symptoms, Diagnosis, Treatment;* 4. *Nutrition and Fitness;* 5. *Emotional and Mental Health;* 6. *Sexuality and Reproduction;* 7. *Drugs, Alcohol, and Tobacco;* 8. *Safety and Environmental Health;* 9. *Health-Care Systems/Cumulative Index.*

The information in the *Macmillan Health Encyclopedia* is clearly presented and easy to find. Entries are arranged in alphabetical order within each volume. An extensive system of cross-referencing directs the reader from a synonym to the main entry (GERMAN MEASLES see RUBELLA) and from one entry to additional information in other entries. Words printed in SMALL CAPITALS ("These substances, found in a number of NONPRESCRIPTION DRUGS . . .") indicate that there is an entry of that name in the volume. Most entries end with a list of "see also" cross-references to related topics. Entries within the same volume have no number (See also ANTI-INFLAMMATORY DRUGS); entries located in another volume include the volume number (See also HYPERTENSION, 3). All topics covered in a volume can be found in the index at the back of the book. There is also a comprehensive index to the set in Volume 9.

The extensive use of illustration includes colorful drawings, photographs, charts, and graphs to supplement and enrich the information presented in the text.

Questions of particular concern to the reader—When should I see a doctor? What are the risk factors? What can I do to prevent an illness?—are indicated by the following marginal notations: Seek Professional Advice, Risk Factors, and Healthy Choices.

Although difficult terms are explained within the context of the entry, each volume of the encyclopedia also has its own GLOSSARY. Located in the front of the book, the glossary provides brief definitions of medical or technical terms with which the reader may not be familiar.

A SUPPLEMENTARY SOURCES section at the back of the book contains a listing of suggested reading material, as well as organizations from which additional information can be obtained.

GLOSSARY

addiction The physical or psychological dependence on chemical substances such as alcohol or other drugs; any habit so strong that it cannot be given up easily.

behavior The way a person acts and responds to the environment.

behaviorism The theory of psychology that focuses on observable behavior and proposes that behavior is determined by learned responses to people, events, situations, and objects within the environment (see PSYCHOLOGY; PSYCHOTHERAPY).

behavior therapy A form of therapy that uses learning and conditioning techniques to change undesirable behavior so that people can function better (see PSYCHOTHERAPY).

cognitive Refers to mental tasks and the processes that enable the mind to accomplish them.

compulsion An irresistible impulse to act or think in a particular way.

culture The knowledge and customs of a certain group of people at a certain time, including beliefs, skills, arts, and institutions.

custom A generally accepted way of doing something, carried on by tradition and social approval.

delusion A false idea that does not correspond to reality.

dependency The physical and/or psychological reliance on something, such as on drugs or alcohol.

drive A state of physical or emotional need that motivates individuals to act in a certain way to fulfill that need.

empathy The identification with and understanding of another individual's situation, feelings, and motives.

environment The elements that surround a person and influence his or her development and behavior, such as family, peer group, ethnic background, culture, and physical surroundings.

euphoria A feeling of great, sometimes exaggerated, happiness and well-being.

feedback The response a person gives to a message and to the sender of the message.

genes Tiny structures in cells that are inherited from parents; they determine an individual's physical and mental characteristics.

heredity The traits—physical, mental, and emotional—that children receive from both of their parents by means of genes; also, the process by which such traits are transmitted through genes.

hormone A chemical substance, such as insulin or estrogen, that stimulates and regulates certain bodily functions.

humanistic therapy A type of therapy that focuses on helping individuals realize their potential, with the assumption that each person is ultimately free to make choices that affect his or her own behavior (see PSYCHOTHERAPY).

involuntary Refers to body functions and actions over which a person has no control.

IQ (intelligence quotient) An intelligence measurement that is derived from a person's score on a standardized intelligence test. The average score for a given age is 100.

modeling The observation and imitation of the behavior of another person.

obsession A preoccupation with a persistent and intrusive idea, image, or desire.

phobia An unreasonable fear of some object, activity, or situation.

psychoanalysis A form of therapy that seeks to help patients uncover and resolve problems and conflicts buried in their unconscious (see PSYCHOTHERAPY).

reinforcement Any consequence of an action that increases the likelihood that the behavior will recur.

response The reaction to a stimulus.

sensory Based on the senses, that is, seeing, hearing, feeling, tasting.

stereotype A set of preconceived beliefs about the characteristics of a group, including the way its members think or act.

stimulus An event, person, idea, or object that is capable of provoking a response.

stressor Anything that causes stress, the body's response to any physical or mental demand made on it (see STRESS).

support group A collection of people with a similar problem or concern who meet to share their difficulties and help one another.

trait A characteristic, either physical, such as brown skin, or behavioral, such as even-temperedness.

traumatic Resulting from a trauma—that is, a physical or emotional shock, usually one that has a lasting effect.

unconscious Memories, motives, and needs that are part of the mind but of which an individual is normally not aware (see MIND).

wellness A state of physical, mental, and social well-being that allows a person to function at his or her best.

ADJUSTMENT

Adjustment is the process of adapting to your surroundings and to the events that occur in your life. Psychologists who study adjustment measure how people cope with change—major and minor—and the STRESS it causes. Any change, whether it is anticipated, such as graduation, or unanticipated, such as the death of a friend, requires adjustment. The ability to adapt to change is dependent on a person's inner resources and support system, as well as his or her view of the change. Some people embrace change. They seek new experiences and look forward to the challenges that they may bring. Other people fear change. These people find change more stressful and adjustment more difficult and painful. Help from supportive family members and counselors can provide relief and shorten the period of time required for the person struggling with adjustment problems.

MAJOR LIFE CHANGES AND EVERYDAY HASSLES

Adjustment involves coping with major life changes as well as minor everyday sources of stress. Examples of each are listed below.

Major life changes	Everyday hassles
Death of spouse	Concerns about weight or physical appearance
Unwanted pregnancy	Health of a family member
Death of parent	Difficulty with roommates
Divorce	Housework or home maintenance
Jail term	Too many things to do
Major injury or illness	Misplaced or lost things
Flunking out of school	Concerns about money, taxes, etc.
Marriage	Concerns about crime
Fired from job	Traffic hassles
New love interest	Regrets about past decisions

Major life changes that require significant adjustment, such as getting married or starting a new job, have been ranked on a stress scale compiled by Thomas Holmes and Richard Rahe in 1967. In recent years, psychologists have suggested that adjusting to life's everyday "hassles" may be as important as adjusting to major events. (See also COPING SKILLS; SELF-EFFICACY; STRESS-MANAGEMENT TECHNIQUES.)

ADULT IDENTITY

Adult identity refers to the sense of self and place in the world that a person develops after adolescence. In the past, many psychologists believed that identity was established during adolescence and remained fixed through adulthood. Today, however, most psychologists agree that

Young Adulthood. *Young adults usually begin establishing a career, a step in accepting responsibility and developing an adult identity.*

an individual's identity is continually reshaped over the course of a lifetime. Even adulthood is characterized by transition and change as people face new challenges and concerns.

There are, however, certain traits that indicate a person has achieved a level of maturity needed to handle the challenges of life successfully. People who have a well-developed sense of self can function independently. They have the confidence to make decisions and the maturity to evaluate those choices. They are aware that their choices will have consequences, and they are prepared to accept those consequences.

Adults who have a secure identity have an established set of personal VALUES, which they rely on to guide their actions and approach to life. Well-adjusted adults are stable enough to establish and maintain both casual and close relationships.

Stages of Adulthood Psychologists recognize several stages in adulthood. In each, different factors are at play in shaping and modifying adult identity. The young adult, who is usually establishing a career, getting married, and perhaps starting a family, develops an increased sense of RESPONSIBILITY and heightened SELF-ESTEEM. During middle adulthood, people assess their accomplishments. For those who view their achievements as positive, middle adulthood may bring increased stability and satisfaction. For those who have missed opportunities and not reached goals, however, it may be a period of frustration and unhappiness. Older adulthood is a period when people usually face a number of transitions as a result of retirement, health crises, and the death of loved ones. Such changes often require adjustments in SELF-IMAGE, habits, ATTITUDES, and behaviors.

HEALTHY CHOICES

Attaining a Healthy Adult Identity It is common for adolescents to believe that participation in such "adult" behaviors as drinking, smoking, or having sex is a way to gain an adult identity. This misconception often results in experimentation with behaviors that can place young people at physical or emotional risk. A healthy adult identity can be attained by learning from past experiences, recognizing and responding to the needs and feelings of others, developing a sense of completeness and inner harmony, expressing EMOTIONS in an appropriate manner, reacting constructively to new challenges, and acting responsibly. Individuals develop this kind of maturity through continual examination of their identity throughout their lives. The reward for achieving a healthy adult identity is a life of great satisfaction and happiness. (See also DEVELOPMENTAL PSYCHOLOGY; SELF-ACTUALIZATION; ADULTHOOD, 1.)

AGGRESSIVENESS

Aggressiveness is a tendency toward any behavior that deliberately causes pain, injury, or harm to others. This behavior can take the form of some type of *physical violence,* such as assault, murder, or rape, or of *verbal aggression,* such as insults or threats.

Although some researchers believe that aggressiveness has a biological basis, most studies indicate that aggressive behavior is generally

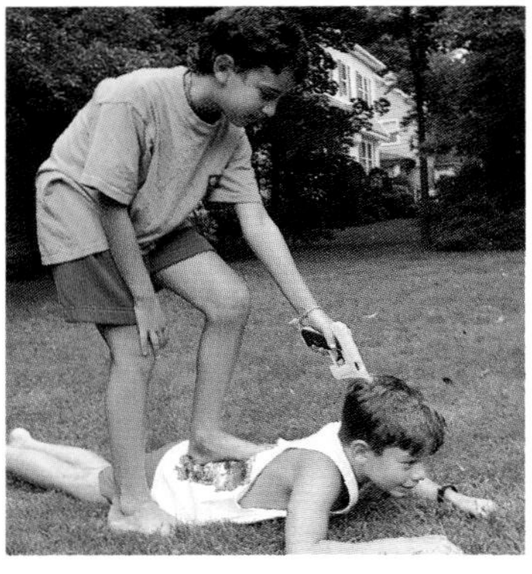

Learning Aggressiveness. *Many types of aggressive behavior are apparently learned, a fact that has caused many people to be concerned about the effects of television violence on children.*

learned. In some cases, it is learned during childhood. For example, children who were abused by parents are more likely to become abusive parents themselves.

Aggressive behavior may also be linked to an individual's situation in life. People who would not behave aggressively under normal circumstances may become aggressive when under extreme stress. A stressful situation such as unemployment or poverty or an inability to cope with everyday problems often results in aggression and violence.

Alcoholism also plays a role in aggressiveness. Drinking is a factor in about half of all murders and in many instances of child abuse and spouse abuse. Alcohol lowers the inhibitions, or internal self-control, of people, which makes them more likely to resort to aggressive or violent behavior.

Psychologists treat aggressive people by helping them recognize their problems and learn new, nonviolent ways of dealing with them. Serious aggression, such as spouse abuse, rape, or murder, is a criminal offense that must be dealt with by law-enforcement agencies. (See also ALCOHOLISM, 7; VIOLENCE, 8.)

ALIENATION

Alienation in Adolescence.

Alienation is a profound feeling of emotional isolation from others. A state of alienation includes a sense of loneliness, being different or misunderstood, and not being liked or needed. Feelings of alienation are common in adolescence, when individuals are undergoing rapid physical and emotional changes. Adolescence is a time when young people begin to define their own identity, which may cause changes in relationships with friends and family members. Although many people experience feelings of alienation from time to time, a deep and prolonged sense of alienation is cause for concern.

Healthy people feel connected to other people and feel that they can affect the course of their lives. An adolescent with a persistent feeling of emotional isolation should consult a school counselor, school psychologist, or other mental health professional. Additional help or information for alienated adolescents or adults may also be obtained through a local crisis hot line or mental health association.

ALTRUISM

see PROSOCIAL BEHAVIOR

AMNESIA

Amnesia is a complete or partial inability to recall information already stored in memory or to memorize new information. A person with amnesia may be unable to remember his or her name, recognize friends or family, or recall certain events; however, general facts such as the names of places or basic skills such as driving are rarely forgotten. Amnesia is caused by damage to the regions of the brain associated with memory. The damage may result from a variety of factors, including head injuries, degenerative diseases such as Alzheimer's disease, drug or alcohol abuse, brain tumors, and strokes.

RISK FACTORS ▶ ▶ ▶ ▶ ▶ ▶

Psychogenic amnesia is amnesia caused by severe psychological stress. It is the mind's way of coping with an extremely disturbing event, such as a violent rape or some other abuse, whether psychological, physical, or both. This amnesia often disappears spontaneously and does not return.

ANGER

Anger is a strong negative EMOTION that arises in response to experiences involving STRESS, frustration, disappointment, unmet expectations, threats, aggression, or prejudice. It is normal for everyone to feel anger from time to time. Anger can have positive effects by spurring people to achievement or positive social action. On the other hand, unresolved or uncontrolled anger can lead to violence and other unhealthy behaviors. Therefore, learning to manage anger and deal with it constructively is important to health, both mental and physical.

Physical Effects of Anger When people feel angry, they experience the anger physically as well as emotionally. Blood pressure typically rises, the heart pounds, and the hands may become sweaty. These physiological effects have led scientists to look for long-term links between anger and disease. The tendency toward hostility and anger is a component of the so-called *type A personality,* which is associated with a risk for heart disease and other disorders. But people who regularly suppress their anger may also be at higher risk for certain diseases. To date, however, scientific evidence establishing anger as a cause for disease is lacking. It may be that the factors contributing to anger—stress, frustration, a lack of control—have as much effect on health as does anger itself.

Faces of Anger. *People the world over tend to produce very similar facial expressions when angry.*

Expressing Anger Most psychologists consider it unhealthy to suppress anger instead of recognizing it and dealing with it. Expressing anger can be done in a way that is either useful or harmful. Using the skills and techniques of ASSERTIVENESS can be a positive, empowering way to express anger. When assertive people express their anger they do it calmly and clearly while leaving room for negotiation and compromise. AGGRESSIVENESS, on the other hand, is a negative, insensitive, or destructive reaction to anger. Aggressive responses such as fighting or blowing up verbally at someone are usually counterproductive.

Managing Anger Experts offer the following advice for coping with anger: When a particular situation arouses anger, try to figure out what about the situation is causing the strong feelings. An angry outburst may stem from feelings that have built up over time, for example, or from some condition or behavior that can be changed. Sometimes anger is caused by frustration, in which case it is important to uncover the source of the frustration and to try to do something about it. For example, a student who puts off a school project until the last minute may become frustrated and angry when it doesn't turn out well; planning enough time to complete projects without pressure may eliminate this frustration in the future.

HEALTHY CHOICES

Try to express your anger calmly and consider how the other person feels. Learn how to manage or avoid the stresses that provoke anger. Exercise, relaxation techniques, and taking a break from a stressful environment can all reduce stress and anger. People who feel angry most of the time or who cannot control their angry outbursts may benefit from PSYCHOTHERAPY or counseling. (See also CONFLICT RESOLUTION; COPING SKILLS; PERSONALITY.)

SEEK PROFESSIONAL ADVICE

ANOREXIA/BULIMIA

Anorexia nervosa and bulimia are two common *eating disorders*. Both are characterized by an irrational fear of obesity. People with *anorexia* typically starve themselves until they are severely underweight—at least 15 percent below the weight expected for their height and age. These individuals have a highly distorted idea of what they look like and continue to diet to the point of starvation. People with *bulimia* binge on enormous quantities of food, then vomit or use laxatives to prevent their bodies from absorbing the calories from the food. These eating disorders are life-threatening conditions that affect as many as 6 percent of the American population.

Anorexia. *In anorexia, a person's body image is highly distorted, and she sees herself as fat no matter how thin she becomes.*

Cases of anorexia and bulimia are most common among white middle- and upper-class adolescent girls and young women, although young men may also have eating disorders. People with eating disorders tend to share certain psychological characteristics: They are often perfectionists and high achievers who have low SELF-ESTEEM. In many cases, their parents expect high levels of achievement from them. These tendencies express themselves as extreme attempts to be thin.

Cultural attitudes also contribute to the pressure to be thin. Americans constantly view images of thin young women in the movies, on television, and in fashion magazines, and they come to believe that they have to be thin to be attractive or successful.

Treatment Without treatment, people with anorexia can starve themselves to death or die of complications such as heart failure. The chronic vomiting in bulimia often results in damage to the digestive system and teeth.

People with eating disorders are treated with a combination of medical attention, nutritional counseling, and PSYCHOTHERAPY. Anorexia is particularly difficult to treat because those with the disorder tend to deny that they have a serious problem, and the denial may be shared by other family members. Anyone who has anorexia or bulimia needs immediate help. Sources of help outside the family include a teacher, counselor, school nurse, or family physician. (See also EATING DISORDERS, 4.)

Antisocial Personality

Antisocial personality disorder, also known as sociopathic or psychopathic personality, is characterized by an extreme disregard for the rights and feelings of others and a lack of normal emotions. People who display this PERSONALITY DISORDER are extremely selfish and feel no guilt or sorrow when they harm others or if others are hurt in any way as a result of their actions. People with antisocial personalities do not lose contact with reality or act bizarrely. In fact, many are quite intelligent, and they may even be charming and friendly. They use these attributes, however, in clever ways to satisfy their own personal needs and desires. They may also use their intelligence to make themselves appear "normal" and capable of expressing emotions that they really do not feel.

Antisocial personality disorder often leads to destructive or criminal behavior. Punishing such behavior seems to do little good, because people with antisocial personalities often fail to learn from experience. No matter how often they are punished, expelled from school, fired from jobs, or imprisoned, they tend to repeat the behaviors that led to their punishment. Signs of the disorder usually appear by age 15 and may include such behaviors as stealing, fighting, delinquency, lying, and a total disregard for responsibility.

Causes The causes of antisocial personality disorder are unknown. Some evidence suggests it may be associated with a faulty AUTONOMIC NERVOUS SYSTEM, which could result in an inability to feel emotions or learn from experience. Other researchers believe that the cause may be rooted in rejection or a lack of affection by parents during childhood. Another theory is that antisocial behaviors develop in childhood through imitation of antisocial parents. (See also AGGRESSIVENESS.)

Anxiety

Anxiety is an emotional state characterized by feelings of worry, apprehension, and fear. These feelings may be accompanied by physical symptoms such as increased heart rate and muscle tension. Anxiety is a normal emotion that everyone experiences at one time or another. In its mild form, it may actually help people accomplish things and improve their performance in a variety of tasks. For example, anxiety before a test, job interview, or athletic match may contribute to a higher level of performance. However, more extreme forms of anxiety may prevent a person from thinking clearly and functioning effectively.

Symptoms A person experiencing anxiety usually has an uneasy feeling that something bad is going to happen. Sometimes such feelings are related to a specific situation, such as worry over health, school, or a social situation. In heightened states of anxiety, a sense of inadequacy, helplessness, and losing control is common. Such feelings may lead to irritability, fatigue, frustration, and SLEEP PROBLEMS.

The physical symptoms associated with more severe anxiety include increased heart rate, perspiration, blushing, muscle tension, tremors in the hands, rapid breathing, dizziness, and gastrointestinal distress. These symptoms are part of the body's *fight-or-flight response* to STRESS, which helps provide the extra strength needed to escape from or overcome some danger or difficult situation. The heightened physical capabilities are a result of increased amounts of chemicals such as epinephrine (adrenaline) flowing into the blood and stimulating the AUTONOMIC NERVOUS SYSTEM. The physical symptoms of anxiety are similar to those of fear. FEAR, however, is a reaction to an identifiable and understandable danger. Anxiety, on the other hand, is generally characterized by the absence of an identifiable cause. A person who experiences anxiety may not know what is causing the distress and the physical symptoms accompanying it. (See also EPINEPHRINE, **1**.)

Causes Psychologists have proposed various theories for the cause of anxiety. Studies focusing on physiological factors have found that anxious individuals usually react more excitedly and adapt more slowly to events than other people do. Psychoanalysts believe that anxiety stems from unresolved childhood experiences and unconscious conflicts. Behavioral psychologists, however, contend that anxiety is a learned response to a stimulus or situation. (See also PSYCHOTHERAPY.)

Treatment Anxiety is often a normal, temporary feeling that passes with time. In such cases, treatment is not usually necessary. Discussing fears and concerns with others is often an effective way to deal with mild anxiety. It is important, however, to understand when anxiety is normal and when it is abnormal and requires treatment. If anxiety persists or interferes with carrying out everyday activities, professional counseling should be sought. Severe, chronic anxiety often requires extensive psychotherapy and, perhaps, the short-term use of some form of antianxiety medication. (See also ANXIETY DISORDERS; DRUG THERAPY.)

ANXIETY DISORDERS

The term *anxiety disorders* refers to a group of conditions in which intense symptoms of ANXIETY and FEAR interfere with the performance of everyday tasks. The basic feature of these disorders is the unreasonable, irrational nature of the fear. The symptoms include feelings of doom, helplessness, frustration, and irritability. Increased heart rate, perspiration, muscle tension, and gastrointestinal distress may also accompany the anxious feelings. Psychologists recognize five types of anxiety disorders: generalized anxiety disorder, panic disorder, phobia, obsessive-compulsive disorder, and post-traumatic stress disorder.

Generalized Anxiety Disorder Generalized anxiety disorder is characterized by long-lasting anxiety that is not focused on anything specific. People with this disorder, also known as free-floating anxiety, are unable to identify the source of their fears and worries. They have trouble relaxing and may experience muscle tension and episodes of dizziness, heart palpitations, stomach pains, and insomnia. People with generalized anxiety are often irritable and impatient, and they may have trouble concentrating. The symptoms may make it difficult to function and carry on with normal activities.

The Scream. *Many artists have attempted to express strong emotions in their works. This 1893 painting by Edvard Munch depicts fear, anxiety, anguish, and despair.*

Panic Disorder People with panic disorder suffer from sudden, brief, and apparently uncontrollable attacks of physical distress characterized by shortness of breath, excessive perspiration, trembling, and heart palpitations. These symptoms are frightening. Although not caused by a specific activity or place, panic attacks may become linked in the individual's mind to a particular situation, causing the individual to avoid that situation in order to prevent the onset of a panic attack. This linkage may ultimately become a phobia. In some cases, panic attacks may have a physiological cause that can be treated.

Phobia A phobia is an unreasonable fear or anxiety associated with a particular object, activity, or situation (see chart: Phobias). The focus of the fear or anxiety may be somewhat dangerous, such as lightning or snakes, or pose no danger at all, such as open spaces or school. By definition, in a phobia, the fear reaction is out of proportion to the danger involved. People with phobias are usually aware of the irrational nature of their fears but are unable to control them except by avoiding the situations or things feared.

Obsessive-Compulsive Disorder Obsessions are persistent and intrusive thoughts. Compulsions are irresistible impulses to act in a particular way. People with obsessive-compulsive disorder dwell on troubling thoughts such as fear of contamination with germs or fantasies of violence. They may also feel compelled to go through certain routines repeatedly, such as washing, counting, or checking that doors are locked.

PHOBIAS

Phobia name	Object or situation feared
Acrophobia	High places
Aerophobia	Flying
Agoraphobia	Open places or leaving the house
Arachnophobia	Spiders
Claustrophobia	Small or closed spaces
Cynophobia	Dogs
Dementophobia	Insanity
Gephyrophobia	Bridges
Hydrophobia	Water
Mysophobia	Dirt or germs
Nyctophobia	Darkness
Ochlophobia	Crowds
Ophidiophobia	Snakes
Pyrophobia	Fire
Thanatophobia	Death
Xenophobia	Strangers

People with this disorder feel powerless to control their thoughts and behaviors. Attempts to resist obsessions or compulsions usually increase tension and anxiety, which can then be relieved only by engaging in the obsession or compulsion.

Post-Traumatic Stress Disorder People who survive a traumatic event, such as a natural disaster or combat, may have long periods of anxiety during which they experience intense fear, feelings of helplessness, insomnia, and recurrent nightmares. Symptoms of POST-TRAUMATIC STRESS DISORDER may continue for years after the traumatic incident and interfere with the person's normal life.

Treating Anxiety Disorders Treatment of anxiety disorders depends on the disorder. Among the treatments used are PSYCHOTHERAPY (including behavior therapy), BEHAVIOR MODIFICATION (such as desensitization), DRUG THERAPY, RELAXATION TRAINING, the development of COPING SKILLS, or some combination of these.

ASSERTIVENESS

Assertiveness is the ability to communicate needs and opinions clearly to others while at the same time respecting their feelings and points of view. Assertiveness is a useful skill for coping with life's stresses and pressures. It helps people deal successfully with conflicts with parents, friends, spouses, bosses, or teachers. This, in turn, reduces the feelings of frustration, ANGER, and ANXIETY that result from STRESS.

Assertiveness is often described as being a healthy midpoint between passiveness and AGGRESSIVENESS. Passive people are generally too timid to express their own needs, feelings, and opinions, or they are too afraid of hurting others' feelings to express their feelings or needs. Aggressive

Assertiveness. *Expressing views and opinions in front of many people requires assertiveness.*

people, on the other hand, tend to push their opinions and demands without regard for the feelings or needs of others. They may intimidate or demean others to get their own way.

Assertive people are not afraid to tell someone no or to disagree, yet they listen to others and show an interest in their comments. Learning to be assertive usually enables people to be more successful at achieving their goals and enhances their SELF-ESTEEM. It promotes healthy interpersonal relationships.

Assertiveness Training Like other social skills, assertiveness can be learned. Some schools, corporations, and other institutions offer assertiveness-training courses to help people change their behavior. These courses often use role-playing exercises to help people become comfortable with assertive communication. They also offer techniques for improving assertiveness, such as rehearsing conversations before a difficult encounter. An employee who is nervous about asking for a raise, for example, can rehearse the conversation beforehand and plan what to say.

HEALTHY CHOICES

It is possible to learn to become more assertive without taking an assertiveness-training class. Begin by practicing on people with whom you are most comfortable. Learn to look assertive by standing straight, smiling, and looking people in the eye. Listen to others attentively, and express an opinion when asked. As confidence increases, volunteering opinions and feelings without waiting to be asked will become easier. (See also COMMUNICATION.)

ATTITUDES

An attitude is a tendency to respond in a positive or negative way to a person, object, idea, or situation. Attitudes are complex states of mind that reflect feelings and beliefs about certain things. They influence many of the choices people make—the products they buy, the friends they choose, the clothes they wear, and all other aspects of their social behavior.

How Attitudes Are Learned Everyone has attitudes—definite ideas and feelings—about many things. Some of these are very important, and some are insignificant. Attitudes are acquired from a variety of sources. One important source is culture, the customs, beliefs, and VALUES shared by society. Culture helps form attitudes about such things as food, love and marriage, and politics. Attitudes are also strongly shaped by family, friends, and peers. As a person matures, attitudes tend to develop based on personal observations of the world and evaluation of information obtained from these observations.

Many attitudes are taken for granted and remain constant, and others will change over time. Some attitudes are adopted or changed in response to the pressure of others. This is known as compliance. You may take on an attitude of someone you admire (identification), or you may adopt an attitude because it is consistent with your basic beliefs (internalization). An attitude about someone that is based on a *stereotype* of the group he or she belongs to is called PREJUDICE.

Attitudes. *People sometimes display their personal and political attitudes on bumper stickers.*

Attitudes and Behavior Although attitudes influence behavior, there is not always a direct relationship between the way people think or feel and what they say or do. This may be because they have conflicting attitudes about something or because they may feel compelled, for some reason, to act in a way that does not fit their attitudes. Sometimes this conflict or inconsistent behavior will cause a change in attitude. For example, a teenage girl may know that smoking poses a great risk to her health, but she may be persuaded by PEER PRESSURE or advertisements to start smoking. She may then change her attitude about smoking to justify her behavior.

Many psychologists explain this kind of change with the theory of *cognitive consistency.* This theory holds that people usually try to have their attitudes match their behavior. Inconsistent attitudes and behavior cause an uncomfortable feeling, called *cognitive dissonance,* which people strive to overcome, often by shifting their beliefs and attitudes to agree with their behavior.

AUTISM

Autism is a severe mental disorder that appears in early childhood. Autistic children are extremely withdrawn and indifferent to their surroundings, and they fail to form relationships with others. They usually have problems with language and impaired intellectual ability. When autistic children are faced with changes in their routine or interference in their activities, they often react with violent temper tantrums. They may also perform repetitive body movements, such as rocking or head banging, and become obsessed with particular objects or ideas. The exact causes of autism are unknown, but evidence seems to suggest a physical basis, possibly some form of brain damage. Although there is no cure for the disorder, a combination of special education, behavioral therapy, and medication can be helpful. (See also PSYCHOTHERAPY.)

Autonomic Nervous System

The autonomic nervous system is the body's mechanism for survival. It is part of the peripheral nervous system, which connects the CENTRAL NERVOUS SYSTEM to the rest of the body (see chart: Divisions of the Peripheral Nervous System). The autonomic nervous system maintains a balance within the body by regulating the involuntary, or automatic, processes of the body. The nerves of this system connect to and regulate internal organs such as the heart, kidneys, and liver; salivary, sweat, and other glands; blood vessels; and the digestive tract. They also regulate breathing and body temperature.

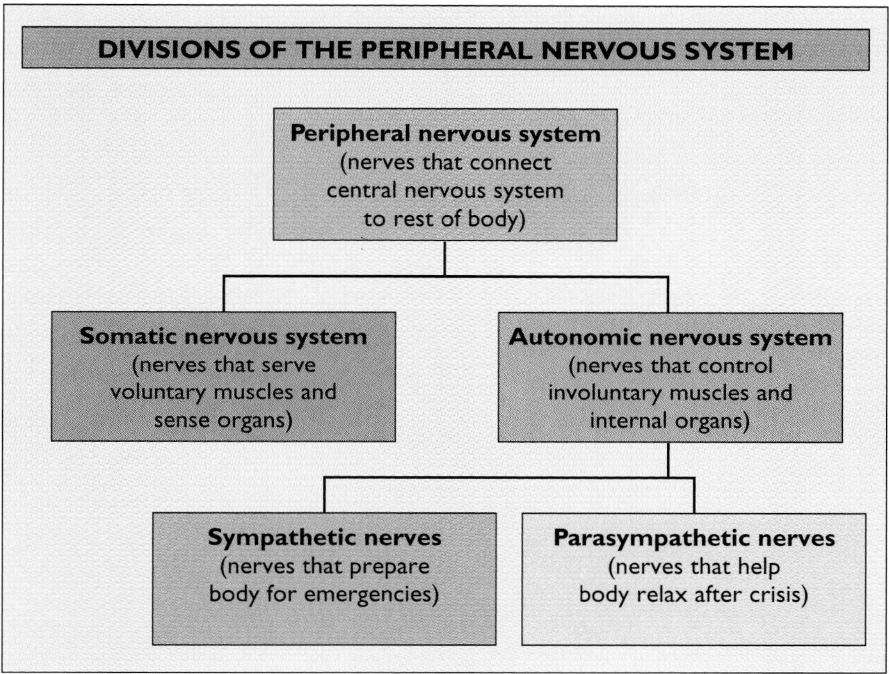

The autonomic nervous system is made up of two distinct parts, which oppose and often balance each other in their regulation of the body's involuntary activities (see chart: Effects of the Autonomic Nervous System). The *sympathetic nervous system* prepares the body to deal with emergencies and to handle other increases in activity. The *parasympathetic nervous system* helps the body return to a resting state after an emergency or other action.

Stress and the Autonomic Nervous System Under normal conditions, when a person's mind and body are relaxed, the parasympathetic nervous system is dominant. It maintains normal heart rate, blood pressure, digestive processes, and other body functions. However, when a person is under any kind of mental or physical STRESS, the sympathetic nervous system takes over and arouses the body. Various changes occur during this response to stress, which is sometimes called the *fight-or-flight response* because it gets the body ready to fight or flee from the source of the stress.

EFFECTS OF THE AUTONOMIC NERVOUS SYSTEM

Part of the body	When body is under stress—the sympathetic nervous system	After stress—the parasympathetic nervous system
Brain	Increases blood flow to brain	Slows blood flow to brain
Eye	Dilates pupil	Contracts pupil
Tear ducts	Stimulates tear glands	Inhibits tear glands
Salivary glands	Decreases production of saliva	Increases production of saliva
Sweat glands	Increases sweating	—
Lungs	Expands bronchi	Contracts bronchi
Heart and circulation	Accelerates heartbeat and raises blood pressure	Slows heartbeat and lowers blood pressure
Stomach, pancreas, and intestine	Slows digestion	Increases digestion
Adrenal gland	Releases epinephrine and norepinephrine	—
Bladder	Relaxes contraction	Contracts bladder
Liver and gallbladder	Stimulates release of sugar by liver	Stimulates gallbladder
Skeletal muscles	Increases blood flow to muscles	Decreases blood flow to muscles

The sympathetic nerves stimulate the release of certain hormones, which increase levels of energy-providing sugar in the blood and encourage the heart to beat faster. Hormones also increase the flow of blood to the brain and skeletal muscles to prepare the body for action. In addition, breathing becomes deeper and more rapid in order to provide oxygen for energy production, the pupils of the eyes dilate to see the danger more clearly, and perspiration increases to regulate body temperature. Muscles beneath the skin contract, causing "goosebumps" when hairs stand on end.

When the stressful situation is over, the parasympathetic nervous system returns the body to normal. It slows heartbeat, lowers blood sugar, and generally returns the body to a state of calm. If the stress is intense and sustained and the body cannot return to normal, however, serious stress-related illnesses such as high blood pressure, heart disease, and ulcers may result. (See also ADRENAL GLANDS, **1**; EPINEPHRINE, **1**; NERVOUS SYSTEM, **1**.)

BEHAVIOR MODIFICATION

Behavior modification is the systematic application of CONDITIONING techniques to change a particular behavior. The techniques used include reward and punishment, aversion, and desensitization. Therapists have used behavior modification to treat a variety of problems ranging from smoking and overeating to shyness and poor study habits.

Behavior Modification Techniques An effective method of changing behavior involves setting up a system of rewards. The individual is given behavior-change goals to achieve, and each time he or she achieves the goal, a reward is given. Consider, for example, a student who finds it hard to study for more than half an hour a night and who wants to increase study time to 2 hours a night. It might be suggested that the student build up to 2 hours a night in half-hour increments and that the student be rewarded each time he or she achieves the goal. The reward might be a special type of food, a movie, or anything else that the student values. The idea is to set realistic goals and to give *positive reinforcement* for continuing a desired behavior.

Punishments for failing to meet goals can also be used to help a person change a behavior. For example, a parent might try to help a child eliminate temper tantrums by walking away each time the child has a tantrum. In general, it has been found that a system of rewards is more effective than a system of punishments.

Another method of behavior modification that is used to change a harmful or undesirable behavior is to replace the usual behavior with a new one. For example, a young woman who has trouble keeping her weight under control knows that she is most likely to munch on junk food when she spends the evening watching TV. To avoid this pattern of behavior, she signs up for an evening dance class, volunteers at the community center, and makes plans to do things with friends several nights a week.

Aversion therapy is another method of modifying behavior. It involves associating the undesirable behavior with something that is unpleasant or even repulsive. For example, smokers may be shown photographs of a cancerous lung when they have the urge to light up a cigarette.

People who want to overcome fear or anxiety that is caused by a particular stimulus, such as snakes or high places, can try *desensitization*. In this method of behavior modification a therapist trains the anxious or fearful person to relax when confronted with the source of the anxiety or fear. While practicing relaxation techniques, a person who fears snakes, for example, may be shown pictures of snakes. Eventually, this person

Desensitization. *With systematic desensitization, people are taught to relax when faced with the object or situation they are afraid of, such as snakes.*

may look at a live snake and then touch it. Because the person has learned gradually to relax in the presence of the feared object, he or she has been able to overcome the fear and anxiety once associated with that object. (See also ANXIETY DISORDERS.)

Behavior Therapy see PSYCHOTHERAPY

Biofeedback

Biofeedback is a relaxation technique in which a person learns to control involuntary functions, such as heart rate and blood pressure, by monitoring those processes on machines. It is useful in helping people treat stress-related disorders such as high blood pressure, migraine and tension headaches, muscle tension, and irregular heartbeat. It has also been used to teach people who have cerebral palsy or who have suffered strokes to gain control of muscle movements.

Biofeedback. *Machines like the one shown here indicate changes in a person's blood pressure and other physiological functions by means of changing tones, flashing lights, or other signals, so that the person can learn to control these functions.*

In a typical biofeedback session, a person is hooked up to a machine that measures heart rate, blood pressure, muscle activity, brain waves, skin perspiration, or body temperature. The machine indicates by a visual or auditory signal what the measurements are. The person may be instructed to perform certain relaxation techniques or to experiment with mental images until he or she is able to cause a change in the measurement—for example, to cause a lower blood pressure reading. The machine signal changes as the bodily function changes, thus "feeding back" information to the person. Gradually, he or she learns to control the internal body processes without direct feedback from signals and machines.

Although biofeedback may be an effective relaxation technique for some people, it does not work for everyone. An additional drawback is that biofeedback requires equipment and trained technicians. Some people find that *meditation* and other types of self-help RELAXATION TRAINING are effective in relieving stress-related disorders without the need for equipment or technical support.

Biological Therapy see PSYCHOTHERAPY

Bipolar Disorder

Bipolar disorder, or manic-depressive illness, is a mental disorder in which a person experiences periods of mania alternating with normal feelings or DEPRESSION. The periods of *mania* are characterized by euphoria (an exaggerated sense of well-being), inflated SELF-ESTEEM, and excessive enthusiasm. A person in the manic phase may also be hyperactive, reckless, and show poor judgment. Such periods may last a few days or several weeks and then shift abruptly to periods of depression. The shifts are usually unrelated to external events. Bipolar disorder tends to appear before age 30, and research suggests that it may be inherited. In severe cases, hospitalization may be necessary, especially during the depressive phase, when there is a danger of SUICIDE. Bipolar disorder is often treated with DRUG THERAPY, which may include lithium to control the severity of the mood swings and antidepressant drugs to treat the depressive phases. (See also ANTIDEPRESSANTS, 7.)

Body Language

Body language is the term used to describe the nonverbal signals that people send to others through their posture, facial expressions, and gestures. Body language is also called *nonverbal communication.* Along with speech and tone of voice, body language helps people communicate with one another. Many people are unaware of their own body language and what it is communicating about their feelings.

Learning to read the body language of others can provide important clues to their state of mind. For example, the body language of a person sitting with arms and legs crossed in a closed, protective posture may indicate defensiveness, nervousness, or anxiety. When that same person sits back, arms unfolded, the body language generally signals a relaxed state of mind and an openness to the ideas of others.

Body language also includes touching and *proximity,* how close one person gets to another. Two people who are in love frequently touch each other. Similarly, happily married spouses tend to stand closer to one another than do unhappily married spouses. On the other hand, moving into someone's personal space uninvited (that is, getting too close) can be perceived as aggressive.

When people lie, their body language sometimes gives them away. If a person says one thing but sends the opposite message with his or her body language, most observers believe the body language. Understanding someone's body language offers clues to that person's thoughts and feelings. This can help you understand better what the person is communicating. (See also COMMUNICATION.)

Body Language. *What does each person's body language tell you about how they are feeling about the conversation they are having?*

BULIMIA

see ANOREXIA/BULIMIA

CENTRAL NERVOUS SYSTEM

The central nervous system (CNS), made up of the brain and spinal cord, is the control center for all human behavior. It enables people to receive information, to make sense of the information, to act on it, and, in some cases, to store it. For example, the CNS allows you to feel and interpret sensations and to move, speak, think, learn, and remember. In addition to its control center function, the central nervous system, in particular the brain, is the source of an individual's unique humanity, PERSONALITY, and EMOTIONS.

The central nervous system acts as a control center when it receives messages from the sense organs, which provide information from outside the body, or from the body's internal organs and tissues. The messages are carried along nerve pathways in the peripheral nervous system, which connects the spinal cord and brain to the rest of the body. The spinal cord transmits sensory information (from the senses) and motor information (from the muscles) between the rest of the body and the brain. The brain, in turn, processes and interprets the information, makes decisions, and conveys instructions to the muscles and glands, again by way of the spinal cord and peripheral nervous system. Some of the basic processes of the central nervous system, such as regulating body temperature, are carried out automatically, or reflexively, without conscious thought.

> Basic functions, such as breathing, movement, appetite, and some emotions, are coordinated by the two lower levels of the brain: the brain stem and the cerebellum.

Functions of the Brain Basic functions, such as breathing, movement, appetite, and some emotions, are coordinated by the two lower levels of the brain: the *brain stem* (which joins the top of the spinal cord to the rest of the brain) and the *cerebellum*. Control of voluntary movement and interpretation of the sensations of sight, sound, and touch are provided by the *cerebrum,* the largest and most highly developed part of the brain.

Sensory and motor information is analyzed and integrated in the *cerebral cortex,* the multilayered, folded covering of the cerebrum. The cortex covers the two hemispheres, or sides, of the cerebrum and is divided into four lobes on each side. Each hemisphere of the cerebrum controls motor and sensory functions for the opposite side of the body, and specific areas in the tissues of the lobes of the cortex control specific motor and sensory activities. The greater the control required by a part of the body, such as the fingers, the larger the amount of cortex devoted to that part.

The sensory and motor areas take up a relatively small part of the cortex (see illustration: Areas of the Cerebral Cortex). The remaining areas are called *association areas,* where information from sensory and motor areas is integrated, interpreted, and acted on. Mental functions such as comprehension, recognition, memory, decision making, carrying out plans, and experiencing conscious emotions also occur in the association areas.

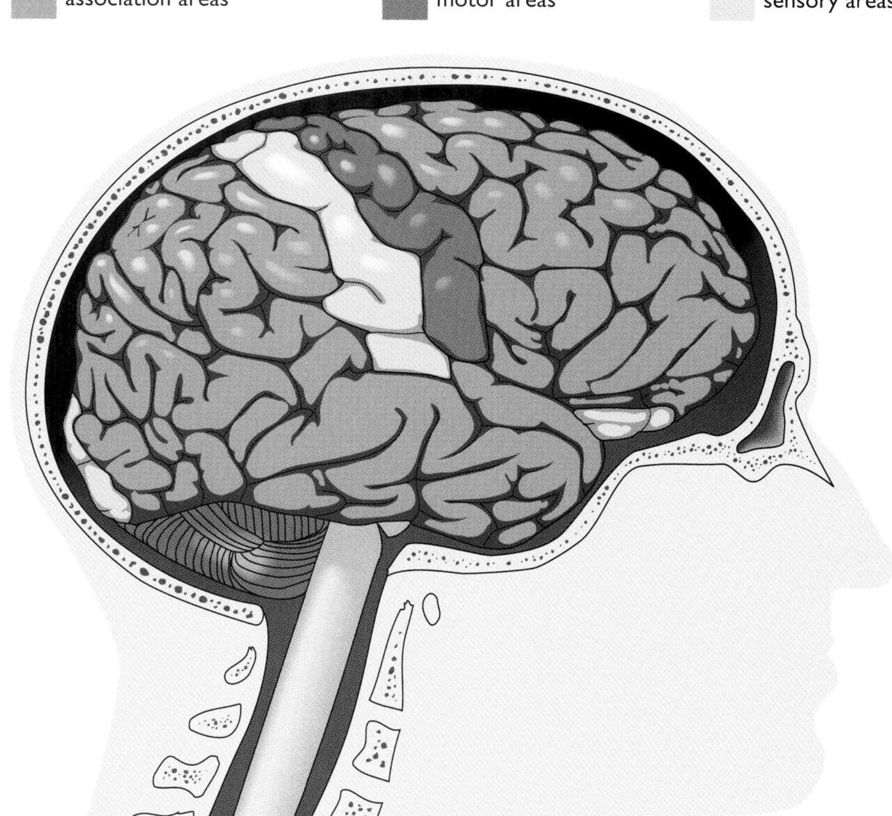

Areas of the Cerebral Cortex. *The association areas make up about three-fourths of the cortex. Besides processing and acting on information from the motor and sensory areas, the association areas affect learning, memory, and other higher-level functions of the brain.*

RISK FACTORS

Damage to the Central Nervous System The central nervous system can be damaged through a traumatic head or spinal cord injury, such as from a traffic or sports accident. It can also be damaged through disease, such as stroke and brain tumor. These injuries can cause physical damage such as muscle weakness and paralysis as well as behavioral changes. Disorders of the nervous system can also be inherited, as may be the case with *dyslexia,* a reading disability. Overuse of drugs and alcohol can also damage the brain by killing brain cells.

If a particular part of the brain is damaged, the sensations and actions controlled by that part can be lost or impaired. For instance, if the parietal lobe, which deals with the sensations of touch and pain, is damaged, a person may not be able to feel the pain from an injury. If the frontal lobe, which affects voluntary emotions and personality, is damaged, the person may experience personality changes, such as going from excitable to passive.

Although some disorders of the brain that affect thought, emotion, or behavior have an organic, or physical, cause, in many cases there is no definite relationship between the mental illness and brain damage. However, mental disorders such as SCHIZOPHRENIA and PARANOIA may possibly be caused by brain disease or other organic factors. (See also AUTONOMIC NERVOUS SYSTEM; PERCEPTION; BRAIN, 1; NERVOUS SYSTEM, 1; SPINAL CORD, 1.)

Circadian Rhythm

Circadian rhythm is the daily pattern of the body's biological functions, including sleep, blood pressure, body temperature, and hormone levels. The term *circadian* comes from the Latin words *circa* (around) and *dies* (day). Circadian rhythms are often referred to as a person's body clock or biological clock.

Most people feel more alert mentally in the mornings. As the day goes on, blood pressure and body temperature increase slightly but energy level declines. Left to itself without any external cues, the human body would function on a 25-hour cycle. However, the body adjusts to a 24-hour day of light and darkness.

Working on rotating shifts and traveling by jet across several time zones disrupts the circadian rhythms of many people. The usual results are SLEEP PROBLEMS and difficulty concentrating during the day. It takes about 2 weeks for the circadian rhythm patterns to become readjusted to a change such as a new work shift or time zone.

Cognitive Therapy

see PSYCHOTHERAPY

Communication

Communication is a two-way process through which people transmit and receive information, ideas, ATTITUDES, and EMOTIONS to one another. Communication between people can involve facial expressions, touch, or the complex interaction involved in language. Good communication is important in building healthy RELATIONSHIPS and in coping with the people and situations encountered in life. On a broader level, communication is a key element in the world of business, in politics, and in the arts.

Elements and Types of Communication The communication process is often broken down into four elements: the sender, or source; the receiver, or audience; the message itself; and feedback, the response of the receiver to the message. *Feedback* is an important, but often unrecognized, part of the communication process. It lets the sender know whether or not a message is getting through and how it is being received.

There are two basic types of communication: verbal and nonverbal. *Verbal communication,* or speech, uses the complex system of symbols that we call language. Language allows us to convey facts, share feelings, and describe abstract ideas from our own imaginations. *Nonverbal communication,* also called BODY LANGUAGE, includes all the ways people communicate without speech—through gestures, posture, facial expressions, and so on. Nonverbal communication provides social clues that people use to understand the behavior of others. A direct gaze, for example, conveys self-assurance and honesty in some cultures. Sometimes there is a conflict between a person's words and the message sent by his or her body language. For example, your friend may say he is interested in the story you are telling, but he looks elsewhere and taps his foot while you are talking, indicating lack of interest.

Communication. *The basic elements of communication are the same no matter how the message is transmitted.*

Effective Communication There are two kinds of messages involved in most communications: one is primarily informational, dealing with facts and perceptions; the other is emotional, dealing with the way people feel about things. The emotional aspect of communication, sharing feelings, plays a vital role in moving a casual friendship toward INTIMACY. An important element in communications involving feelings is *empathy,* the ability to put yourself in the other person's place and understand what that person feels.

Of course, good communication is important in all types of relationships. It depends on each person involved in the two-way process performing his or her role, in other words, on the sender being a good communicator and the receiver being a good listener. The following tips may help you improve your communication skills.

Being a good communicator means being understood. Get straight to the point, speak clearly, and express feelings and facts as precisely as possible. Address the issue directly, while not attacking or putting the blame on others. Be open to people's beliefs and feelings. Understanding other points of view will help in planning what to say, how best to say it, and what kind of feedback to expect. Listen to feedback to see whether your message is being received and how it is being interpreted.

HEALTHY CHOICES

Being a good listener means trying to understand the message and showing understanding. Encourage other people to talk, pay attention to what they have to say, and offer appropriate feedback. Try to interpret nonverbal as well as verbal messages; sometimes what is *not* being said is important. Ask for clarification if you are not sure what others are trying to communicate.

Acquiring these skills may help a person overcome many of the pitfalls that can occur at all levels of communication—problems such as misunderstanding, false assumptions, and differences of personality and opinion. Communication is always a two-way process; listening for the other person's point of view as well as clearly expressing your own leads to effective communication. (See also ASSERTIVENESS; CONFLICT RESOLUTION; SOCIAL SKILLS.)

CONCEPT

Concepts are the mental images that individuals use to classify and organize people, objects, and events with similar characteristics. Concepts help organize the world and make it more understandable. The ability to

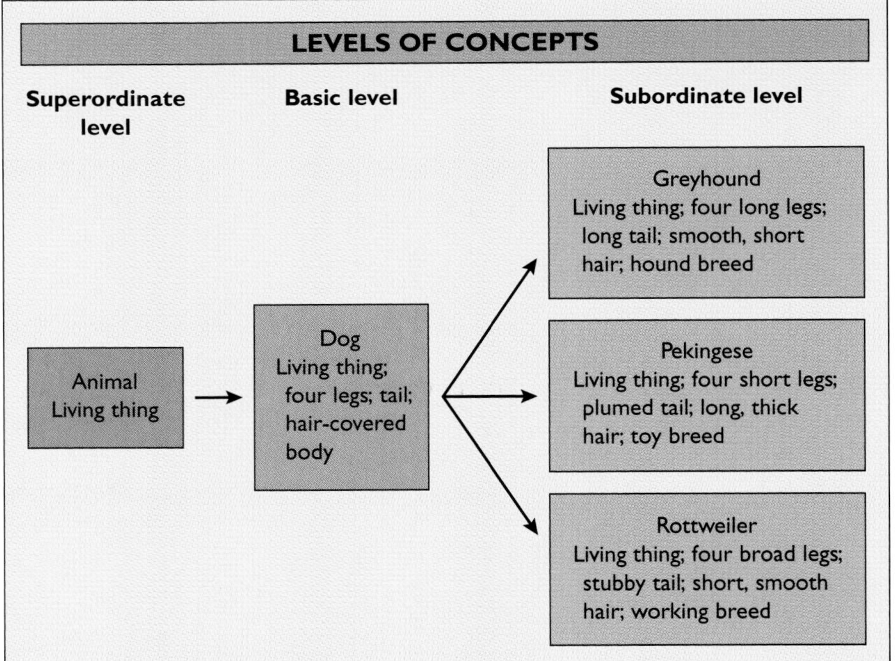

Levels of Concepts. *Members of basic-level concepts, such as dogs, chairs, and cars, are the easiest to categorize and are usually learned first by children.*

form concepts allows people to think and learn, to make decisions, to reason and solve problems, and to comprehend and communicate with language.

Without concepts, people would need a different name for every object and idea. Fortunately, the mind simplifies things by grouping similar objects into concepts. The object you read your history assignment in yesterday and the object you are reading from now are both *books*. Concepts such as book, shirt, chair, car, flower, and so on that people use in general, everyday conversation are called *basic-level concepts*. Concepts are also formed at broader levels (books are a type of *reading matter*) and at more specific levels (*textbooks, encyclopedias,* and *romance novels* are types of books) (see chart: Levels of Concepts).

How Concepts Are Learned People acquire concepts by LEARNING from others or by observing the world directly. Children begin at a young age to learn basic concepts from their parents. A parent points to a dog, for example, and says "dog"; the child gradually learns what features define *dog*—four feet, fur, a tail. If the child then tries to apply the same label to a cat, the child will be corrected and told that this animal is a cat. The child will eventually figure out that although cats have four feet, fur, and a tail, they are smaller, have a different shape, and have prominent whiskers. The shape and whiskers serve as *defining attributes* (characteristics) that help the child recognize a cat the next time the child sees one.

Several theories have emerged to explain how people form concepts. One theory suggests that people retain a mental list of defining attributes for each concept. When encountering a new object or idea, a person compares its features with those of an already known concept. For many everyday concepts, however, defining attributes are often vague. The defining attributes of book, for example, would have to be flexible enough to include a dictionary, a notebook, and a novel recorded on cassette.

Another theory suggests that people organize and recognize most ordinary concepts in terms of *prototypes*, or the examples that best represent particular things. A dictionary and notebook are both books, but the dictionary is probably closer to your image of a typical book than the notebook is. According to this theory, the more closely an object fits a prototype you have formed, the more readily you will include it as a member of its category.

CONDITIONING

Conditioning, also called associative learning, is a type of learning that occurs when an association is made between a stimulus (event, person, or object) and a certain response (behavior). *Classical conditioning*, which affects involuntary responses (those over which you have no control), and *operant conditioning*, which involves voluntary (or intentional) responses, are the two main types of conditioning.

Classical Conditioning Ivan Pavlov, a Russian physiologist who won the Nobel Prize in 1904 for his study of the digestive process, discovered the principle of classical (also called respondent) conditioning. During his research on how the stomach prepares to digest food, Pavlov noticed that the dogs he used for research would start salivating even at the sight or smell of food. Curious about this response, Pavlov began to conduct experiments to identify conditions that produced salivation (see illustration: Pavlov's Classical Conditioning Experiment). The experiment involved striking a tuning fork immediately before placing meat powder on a dog's tongue. After repeating this a number of times, the dog salivated when he heard the tuning fork, even when the food was not given. The process of teaching the dog a new connection between the stimulus

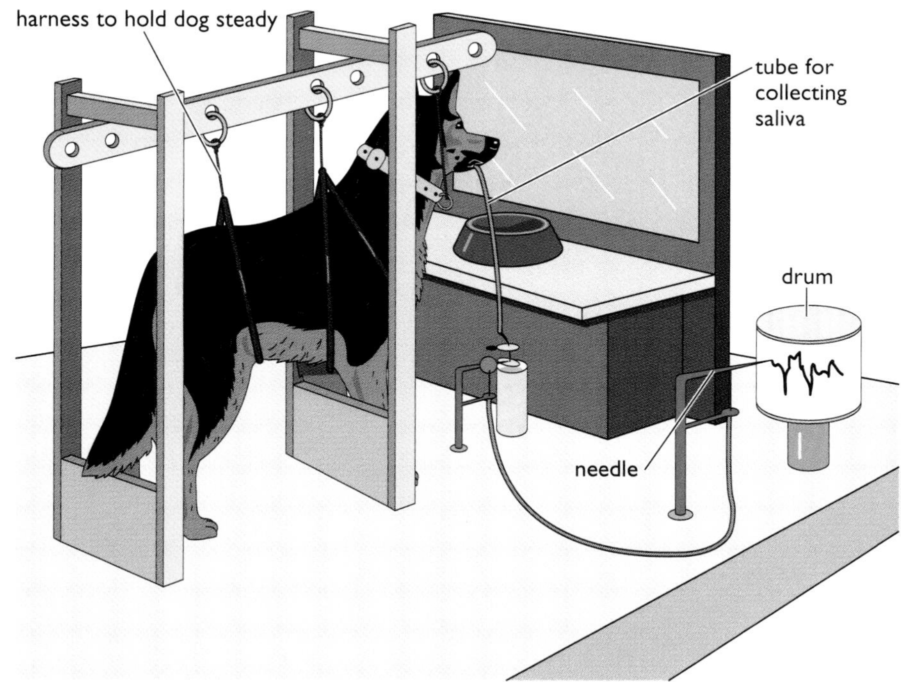

Pavlov's Classical Conditioning Experiment. *To test the dog's response to various stimuli such as food or the sound of a tuning fork, Pavlov attached a tube to the dog's mouth. When drops of saliva flowed down the tube, they activated a needle, which recorded the information on a revolving drum.*

Operant Conditioning. *Animals can be taught, through receiving positive reinforcement of food, to perform actions that they would not instinctively do, such as a killer whale's jumping on command.*

(sound of the tuning fork) and the response (salivation) became known as classical conditioning.

Classical Conditioning and Human Behavior Examples of classical conditioning are commonplace in everyday life. For instance, perhaps you have experienced a reaction similar to that of Pavlov's dogs when you are hungry: Looking at food or reading a menu will make you start to salivate. Besides causing this type of involuntary sensory behavior, classical conditioning affects emotional responses. For example, the fear experienced by soldiers in a war can be felt again even years later when the men and women are exposed to war sounds or sights.

Operant Conditioning American psychologists, notably B. F. Skinner, believed that Pavlov's model of classical conditioning explained involuntary behavior, but it could not explain most complex voluntary responses. Skinner proposed instead the theory of operant conditioning, in which a behavior is learned because of the effect or consequences of the behavior. Any outcome or consequence of an action that increases the likelihood that the behavior will recur is called a *reinforcement.* Behavior is likely to be repeated if it is followed by a reward or pleasurable experience (positive reinforcement) or if by doing it an unpleasant stimulus is halted or avoided (negative reinforcement). A behavior will probably not be repeated if it is followed by an unpleasant experience (punishment). In order for reinforcement to be most effective, it must follow the desired behavior immediately so that the connection between action and reward or punishment is clearly made. Through operant conditioning, a dog can be taught to "shake hands" if it is given a biscuit (positive reinforcement) every time it lifts its paw (see illustration: Operant Conditioning).

Operant Conditioning and Human Behavior An understanding of operant behavior can help people find better ways to teach children and to help change their own behavior. For example, a person who decides to eat a healthy diet and exercise regularly in an attempt to lose weight is more likely to continue these behaviors if the action is rewarded. Loss of weight, compliments from friends, and a good feeling about oneself all provide positive reinforcement.

Punishment, which involves applying a negative stimulus such as spanking or withdrawing a positive stimulus such as a child's allowance, is an aspect of operant conditioning that is often misused. It often does not get the desired result. Because punishment does not cause an unwanted behavior to be unlearned, it often reappears after punishment. Also, a person may be angry and resentful of the punishment and may perform other types of negative, undesirable behavior. In other cases, punishment actually reinforces undesired behavior because the person who is misbehaving may see punishment as a form of attention. Punishment should be used cautiously and only in extreme cases. Those in authority should rely rather on positive reinforcement to teach desired behavior. (See also BEHAVIOR MODIFICATION; LEARNING.)

Conflict Resolution

Conflict resolution is the process of settling a disagreement or dispute between people to the mutual satisfaction of the parties concerned. In itself, conflict is not a bad thing. Conflicts arise in all close RELATIONSHIPS; they are inevitable because people are bound to differ at some point over ideas, needs, or goals. Yet unresolved conflicts are a source of STRESS and can threaten or destroy a relationship. Settling a conflict successfully can make the relationship stronger by helping partners understand each other better and realize that conflict does not automatically result in rejection or punishment. It also helps them gain the skills necessary to solve future conflicts.

The Conflict Resolution Process Conflict resolution involves skills in *negotiation* and problem solving. The first step is to discuss the conflict calmly, examining both sides of the issue. Next, the parties may have to make *compromises;* that is, each person agrees to give up something in return for getting something else. When people are unable to resolve a conflict themselves, they may consult a professional mediator, a marriage counselor, or a family therapist. These specialists try to help the individuals involved in conflict define the issues or clarify feelings and search for solutions.

Conflict Resolution. *Conflicts between groups of people are often negotiated in meetings involving representatives of the groups, often with the aid of a mediator.*

Resolving Conflicts Successfully There are several important principles to remember in seeking to resolve conflicts. One is to keep the discussion focused on the disagreement and to avoid personal attacks. Using "I" statements such as "I feel . . ." is preferable to using "you" statements that blame. It is also important for individuals to control their emotions, even if they feel very angry. A "cooling off" period between the initial conflict and resolution efforts may be necessary. Another person should never be attacked physically or verbally. If the emotional level gets too intense, taking a break may help individuals calm down.

HEALTHY CHOICES

A conflict can be resolved only if each person respects the other person's point of view and listens carefully to all arguments. Each partner must be willing to make some compromises. Often it will be necessary for both individuals to apologize for wrong actions. When a conflict seems impossible to solve, seeking outside help is the best solution. (See also ANGER; COMMUNICATION.)

CONFORMITY

Conformity refers to the tendency of individuals to match their ATTITUDES and behaviors to those of others. People who conform adopt the appearance, opinions, or behaviors of others in order to be accepted or approved by the group. Group pressure can exert a powerful influence—which can be positive or negative—on individuals. Studies have found that this influence varies according to the size of the group, the amount of agreement within it, and the degree to which nonconformity can be hidden. The smaller the group and the more agreement among its members, the greater its influence. The more anonymity a person has within a group, the less the need to conform. Other factors that tend to increase conformity are being lower in status than other group members and having low SELF-ESTEEM.

Experts have identified several types of conformity. *Compliance* occurs when someone outwardly conforms to a group while inwardly maintaining his or her own opinions. People often comply out of fear of

Conforming to a Group. *Adolescents often show a strong tendency to conform to the clothing styles of their peer group.*

punishment or persecution or from a fear of being excluded by the group. When threats are lifted, these individuals often stop complying. A second type of conformity is *identification,* a tendency to conform because of admiration for others and a desire to be like them. A third type of conformity, *internalization,* occurs when a person truly begins to accept the views of others as appropriate and correct. People who internalize the views of others are more likely to continue to conform when they are away from the group. Some people consider conformity to be bad because it weakens individuality and independence. Others, however, believe it has positive effects, including the encouragement for people to perform socially acceptable behaviors and actions. (See also PEER PRESSURE; PROSOCIAL BEHAVIOR.)

COPING SKILLS

Coping skills are the techniques individuals use to help them deal with challenges and change in order to avoid or minimize STRESS. Coping skills include both ways of thinking and ways of behaving. Because stress is a normal part of life, coping skills are essential to good health. Some coping skills focus on preventing stress; others help you deal with it when it cannot be avoided.

Preventing Stress Coping effectively often involves preventing stress or preparing for it in such a way as to diminish its effects. Among the techniques for preventing stress are good personal management skills such as time management. *Time management* helps people handle a number of tasks in a given period of time. It involves budgeting time—planning for projects ahead of time and breaking large tasks into smaller, more manageable ones—and establishing priorities—ranking tasks according to their urgency and importance.

HEALTHY CHOICES

A healthy lifestyle also affects how well a person prevents or handles stress. Regular exercise helps the body eliminate the physical byproducts of stress, improves overall fitness, and increases the energy level and sense of well-being. Good nutrition provides the fuel the body needs to function adequately during times of stress.

Coping with Stress When stress cannot be prevented or adequately prepared for, a variety of coping strategies may be useful. These include maintaining a *positive outlook,* which means viewing change as a challenge to be overcome rather than an event designed to bring defeat. The loss of a job, for example, could be seen as an opportunity to train for a more satisfying career, open a business, or move to a new, more interesting location.

Another coping strategy is to face a source of stress head on, using problem-solving skills to eliminate problems. *Problem solving* is the process of identifying a problem, finding and evaluating solution alternatives, and choosing a course of action from among the alternatives. Anticipating problems and solving them promptly greatly reduces the stress they can cause.

Another important coping technique is to find strength in positive RELATIONSHIPS. Friends and family members can listen and offer support during difficult times. Some individuals find help through *support groups,*

Setting Priorities. *When a number of tasks confront you, sitting down and ranking them in order of importance can help you plan how to accomplish the tasks that are most important to you.*

groups organized to help with specific types of problems such as alcoholism and weight control. Through support groups, individuals can find ways to cope with their problems and help others cope as well. RELAXATION TRAINING techniques, such as progressive relaxation and meditation, help people handle the physical and emotional effects of stress.

Coping successfully with challenges and change helps build SELF-EFFICACY, self-confidence, and a sense of capability. When a stressful situation arises, it is best to deal with it promptly. However, it is also important to be realistic about what you *can* do and to recognize that you can't do everything. (See also CONFLICT RESOLUTION; FRIENDSHIP; STRESS-MANAGEMENT TECHNIQUES.)

CREATIVITY

Creative Expression. *People can derive a great deal of satisfaction from their creative endeavors.*

Creativity is the ability to produce ideas or solve problems in ways that produce original and sometimes valuable results. Many creative people are drawn to fields such as scientific research and the arts, including painting, writing, music, and theater. However, creative thinking and expression can occur on many levels, in many different ways, and in many types of endeavor.

Most creative people are intelligent, curious, and persistent in pursuing their ideas. Some researchers believe creative people are more talented than are others at divergent thinking. *Divergent thinking* is the ability to generate a number of new solutions to a single problem rather than to come up with one conventional solution. Another quality common to creative people is *insight,* that is, being able to size up and understand a problem quickly.

Although some people are consistently more creative than others, researchers believe that nearly all people can enhance their level of creativity with the encouragement of others. Thinking creatively usually gives individuals a deep sense of satisfaction, a knowledge that their work is an expression of self and for that reason highly meaningful. (See also SELF-ACTUALIZATION.)

Crisis Intervention

Crisis intervention is the process of providing immediate help to a person or family experiencing an extremely stressful situation or a mental health emergency. Crisis-intervention programs deal with such problems as drug and alcohol abuse, family violence, SUICIDE attempts, and runaway children. The purpose of crisis intervention is to deal with an immediate crisis until the person or family can be directed to an appropriate place for long-term care.

Shelter and Support. *Community crisis centers, such as those for abused women, are staffed by counselors trained to deal with individuals' emotional turmoil during an emergency.*

Crisis intervention may be provided by community or school district social service agencies, hospital emergency rooms, the police department, and special telephone hot lines. A telephone *hot line* enables individuals who are in trouble to call and receive immediate support and counseling. Hot lines are usually operated around the clock and are staffed by trained volunteers.

All crisis-intervention programs are designed to offer support, encouragement, and a listening ear first. Program workers then try to help the troubled person or family look realistically at the crisis situation and find ways to handle it constructively. Finally, crisis-intervention programs try to refer people in trouble to community services that can provide long-term counseling programs or to other professional help.

Crisis-intervention programs are often listed in local telephone directories under "Crisis-Intervention Services," under local "Emergency Numbers," within the section on government services, or under the problem itself such as "Rape" or "Suicide." Local mental health agencies, school counselors or psychologists, hospitals, and the police department can also provide information on crisis-intervention programs.

Defense Mechanism

A defense mechanism is a mental strategy that people use to protect themselves emotionally from stressful situations and to bolster their SELF-IMAGE when it is threatened. Defense mechanisms lessen negative feelings by allowing people to deny or distort reality unconsciously, so that it does not conflict with their needs or expectations. Everyone uses defense mechanisms now and then to cope with the STRESSES in their lives, but depending on them too much can impair a person's ability to function and cause psychological problems.

Kinds of Defense Mechanisms Sigmund Freud, the founder of psychoanalysis, was the first to recognize defense mechanisms. According to Freud, the most fundamental defense mechanism is *repression.* In repression, people get rid of their anxiety-provoking thoughts, feelings, and memories by pushing them into their *unconscious.* Then they are unaware of having such thoughts or memories. In addition, repressed thoughts cannot be brought to the conscious level easily. For example, a child who faced a trauma such as witnessing a death may block the incident from his or her consciousness and be unable to remember the event. Forgetting a dental appointment or homework assignment may also be due to repression.

Denial is a defense mechanism similar to repression. It occurs when people refuse to recognize a threatening idea or action. People who have been told that they are dying typically undergo a period of denial before eventually facing their illness.

Regression is reacting to threatening thoughts or feelings by behaving in a manner appropriate to an earlier stage of development. A teenager who pouts or throws a temper tantrum when he does not get his way is showing regression.

Displacement occurs when people who cannot express their emotions in one situation vent them inappropriately in other situations. A student who cannot express anger to a teacher may go home and yell at a sister or brother. *Sublimation* is a healthy form of displacement in which the person finds a socially acceptable or constructive way of dealing with his or her emotions. Instead of yelling at a younger sister, the student might work off feelings of anger toward the teacher by exercising, drawing, or writing a story.

Repression. *Soldiers who have been in combat may repress incidents that were especially traumatic, making it difficult for them to adjust to peacetime.*

Projection occurs when people attribute their unacceptable feelings or thoughts to others. A woman who fears she is suffering from a mental illness may instead insist that her husband is mentally ill. *Reaction formation* is a similar defense mechanism. In it, people adopt exactly the opposite feelings and behaviors from the ones that are causing them anxiety. People who crusade zealously against homosexuality may be afraid of their own homosexual feelings.

In *depersonalization,* people—usually because they cannot accept their own fears and weaknesses—refuse to recognize that other people are human. Directed against groups of people, depersonalization plays an important role in racism, ethnic conflict, sexism, and other kinds of discrimination. It has been used to justify the slavery, oppression, and killing of entire groups because of their race or ethnic background.

Rationalization is a defense mechanism in which people substitute socially acceptable reasons for thoughts or actions that have unacceptable motives. Some people cheat on tests because, they tell themselves, everybody else does it.

Benefits and Dangers of Defense Mechanisms Used occasionally, defense mechanisms are normal and sometimes healthy strategies for dealing with stress. By reducing feelings of anxiety, defense mechanisms give people time to face their problems and enable them to deal more effectively with their responsibilities, such as school or work. Defense mechanisms become a problem, however, when a person relies on them as the only means of coping with conflict and stress. Overuse of defense mechanisms prevents the person from acknowledging and reducing the source of anxiety and results in behavior that appears irrational and confusing to others. (See also ANXIETY; COPING SKILLS; MIND; SELF-EFFICACY.)

DEPRESSION

Depression is a psychological state in which people feel sadness, guilt, and hopelessness. Everyone experiences depression occasionally, but the feelings are usually mild and temporary. Depression becomes a serious mental disorder when it becomes severe, lasts for a long time, and interferes with normal functioning. Between 10 and 15 percent of Americans

Major Depression. *People who have major depression feel a profound unhappiness and a general loss of interest in life.*

will experience a severe bout of depression at least once in their lives, but most will recover completely.

Minor Depression Minor (or mild) depression may be experienced by people as a result of psychological STRESS, such as breaking up with a loved one, losing a job, or failing a test in school. Symptoms of this condition, which is sometimes called the common cold of psychological disorders, can include moodiness, uncontrollable crying, anxiety, and pessimism.

Major Depression and Bipolar Disorder More severe types of depressive illnesses are classified by psychologists as *mood disorders* (or affective disorders). The two main types of mood disorders are major depression and bipolar disorder.

Major depression, also called unipolar depression, causes intense feelings of melancholy, helplessness, loss of self-esteem, and guilt. Major depression usually develops very gradually and lasts a long time, although it may begin suddenly when associated with severe psychological stress. The illness can lead to a variety of physical symptoms including loss of appetite, loss of weight, headaches, extreme lethargy or agitation, insomnia, fatigue, and loss of concentration. People with major depression lose all zest for life, and many contemplate committing SUICIDE. More than 80 percent of the people who commit suicide each year are believed to have been experiencing major depression at the time of their deaths.

RISK FACTORS ▶ ▶ ▶ ▶ ▶ ▶

Psychological traumas, such as divorce or a death in the family, trigger about half of all major depressions. Others are brought on by drug or alcohol abuse or by physical illnesses, such as cancer and heart disease. Hormonal imbalance related to a thyroid condition, to premenstrual syndrome, and to bodily changes after childbirth can also cause depression. Heredity may be a factor in depressions that seem to have no apparent cause.

Another factor in some types of depression may be seasonal changes. Some people feel depressed during the winter months and seem to bounce back during the spring or summer. This phenomenon has come to be called *seasonal affective disorder* (SAD). Although the research on SAD is far from complete, some researchers have produced considerable mood improvement in people with winter depression by exposing them to artificial sunlight.

BIPOLAR DISORDER, also known as manic-depressive illness, is a much less common but very serious type of mood disorder. It is characterized by widely varying mood swings from mania—extreme euphoria (exaggerated sense of well-being) and hyperactivity—to depression—deep sadness and loss of interest in life. The causes of bipolar disorder are not clear, but heredity seems to be a significant factor.

Treatment People who have minor, short-term depression can help themselves by exercising, distracting themselves with hobbies, and expressing their feelings to supportive family and friends.

Most cases of chronic and major depression can be treated by psychotherapy and antidepressant drugs. Severe depression is sometimes treated with ELECTROCONVULSIVE THERAPY, also called shock therapy. It is usually used only when DRUG THERAPY has not worked. Severely depressed people who are having suicidal thoughts may need to be hospitalized for their own protection. With treatment, most people can recover completely from most depressions. (See also ALIENATION.)

DEVELOPMENTAL PSYCHOLOGY

Developmental psychology is the study of the way human behavior changes as people grow, mature, and learn from birth through adulthood. It includes theories about intellectual, emotional, and moral development. Developmental psychologists look for patterns of thinking and behaving that are found in most children. They study the roles that both HEREDITY AND ENVIRONMENT play in the growth of skills and abilities. People who work with children apply the principles of developmental psychology to tasks as diverse as designing teaching materials and suggesting methods of discipline. Developmental principles can also help adults understand themselves and the people around them.

Intellectual Development One of the pioneers in the study of intellectual, or cognitive, development was Jean Piaget (pyah ZHAY). In the 1920s, Piaget noticed that when children were given intelligence tests, there were interesting patterns in their wrong answers. On investigating, he found that children of a certain age tended to make similar mistakes that differed from those made by younger and older children. He decided that children think in fundamentally different ways than adults do. Furthermore, as children grow, they pass through stages; in each stage their way of thinking is different. In other words, children do far more than just acquire more facts as they mature. They acquire whole new ways of thinking.

Piaget organized his ideas into a theory of intellectual development. He identified four stages that mark the significant changes in the way a

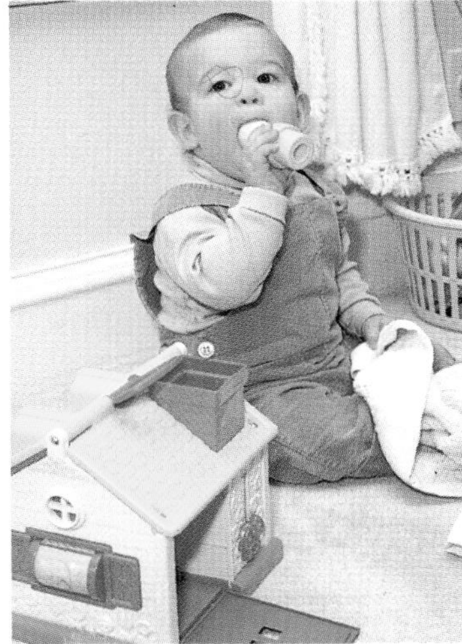

Intellectual Development. *The infant at the top is in the sensorimotor stage, in which the world is explored through the senses. The child at the bottom is in the concrete operational stage, during which mathematical and scientific concepts can be understood.*

child sees the world. He believed that all children go through the same stages in the same order.

- During the *sensorimotor stage,* from birth to age 2, children explore the world through their senses. An infant shaking a rattle and trying to put it in her mouth is an example of this.
- In the *preoperational stage,* ages 2 to 7, children begin to use images and symbols, including language, but cannot reason with logic. Children become able to pretend, but they do not distinguish well between the real and the imagined.
- During the *concrete operational stage,* ages 7 to 11, children develop logical thought about physical objects. When shown a ball of clay, for example, a child at this stage understands that the quantity of clay does not change when the ball is rolled into a long cylinder. A preoperational child will usually say that the cylinder has more clay than the ball.
- In the *formal operational stage,* from age 11 to adulthood, abstract thinking appears. Adolescents' developing ability to reason formally often reveals itself in strong opinions on social or political issues.

Social and Emotional Development In the 1950s, Erik Erikson proposed a theory about how people develop an identity and learn about social relationships. He described a series of eight social and emotional stages that people go through in their lives. The choices made at each stage become part of the emotional background of the person.

The first of Erikson's stages, which he labeled *basic trust versus mistrust,* involves learning basic trust. If an infant's needs are satisfied, the infant will come to believe that the world is good. Otherwise, the infant will learn to expect little in the way of comfort and support. As infants become toddlers, they need to develop a sense of independence. When you see children trying to dress themselves, they are at this stage, which Erikson termed *autonomy versus shame and doubt.* In Erikson's view, failing at one stage makes it difficult for a child to succeed at the next stage. Infants who have learned to mistrust others may not feel confident enough to try out their independence as toddlers. Instead, they will learn self-doubt and shame.

At the next stage (*initiative versus guilt*), preschool-aged children expand on their independence and begin to initiate play with peers and imagine themselves in adult roles. Their behavior is not always appropriate, however, and conflicts that arise with peers or family may cause guilt. Excessive guilt can curb further initiative. At the fourth stage (*industry versus inferiority*), school-aged children apply themselves to learning skills inside and outside of school. Mastering skills helps children feel competent and self-assured; those who do not succeed at certain skills may feel inferior and may work less hard.

According to Erikson, the major issue during the adolescent stage (*identity versus role confusion*) is developing a personal identity—a sense of self. Failure to develop this sense may result in confusion about such things as career choices or sexual identity. Passage to adulthood brings on further stages, each with its own challenges and choices. In Erikson's terms, these stages are *intimacy* (gaining companionship) *versus isolation;*

generativity (being productive and/or raising a family) *versus stagnation;* and, in old age, *integrity* (viewing one's life as productive and satisfying) *versus despair.* Erikson's theory helps to explain how people develop a particular ADULT IDENTITY and highlights the emotional issues faced throughout the life span.

Lawrence Kohlberg proposed a theory about how people learn to think about right and wrong. His theory divided moral development into a series of stages.

Moral Development In the 1970s, Lawrence Kohlberg proposed a theory about how people learn to think about right and wrong. His theory divided moral development into a series of stages. In his research, Kohlberg presented people of all ages with stories in which the characters face a moral choice. He asked each person to decide which choice was best, and noted their reasoning. Kohlberg believed that the kind of reasoning showed the person's level of moral development.

Kohlberg identified three basic levels of moral development; each level is divided into two stages. At the *preconventional level,* moral choices are made in order to avoid punishment or gain a concrete reward. Children at this level make decisions based on whether or not they will "get in trouble." At the *conventional level,* moral issues are decided in terms of gaining approval (or avoiding disapproval) and following society's rules. At the *postconventional level,* people use universal ethical principles of justice and rights to make decisions. According to Kohlberg, people move through the levels at their own rate; some adults may never reach the third stage, the postconventional level.

Physical growth, maturation, and learning all contribute to the development of an individual throughout life. Developmental psychologists try to identify the fixed stages that people move through during their life span. Some theories overlap, so that a significant intellectual development seems to happen at the same time as a new emotional stage. The precise ages at which changes occur may vary. In addition, adults sometimes use a mixture of lower- and higher-level skills. Despite these individual differences, the principles of developmental psychology provide a useful framework for understanding changes in human behavior over time. (See also PSYCHOLOGY; SELF-IMAGE; CHILD DEVELOPMENT, 1.)

DIVORCE

Divorce is the legal ending of a marriage. Psychologically, divorce is one of the most traumatic of life's events, involving drastic changes in a person's way of living. Divorced people experience many painful emotions and major changes in RELATIONSHIPS with FAMILY and friends. Because marriage generally starts with high expectations for a lifetime of joy and happiness, its end through divorce is especially devastating. Each year more than 1 million couples divorce.

Why Couples Divorce There are many reasons why a couple might seek a divorce. One of the most common reasons is the end of romantic love. LOVE relationships typically follow a pattern that begins with intense, romantic love and gradually broadens over a period of years into a deeper, yet less physically intense partnership. Divorce is often the result when the individuals in a couple expect romantic love to continue forever and do not make the transition to a deeper kind of love. A marriage

The Decision to Divorce. *Constant quarreling may lead a couple to consider dissolving a marriage through divorce.*

may also end if the partners bring unrealistic expectations into a marriage and gradually become disappointed when the marriage does not live up to those expectations.

Marriages may end when one partner's views of the proper role of husband or wife changes and starts to conflict with the expectations of the other partner. In some cases, divorce is the result of a long period of spouse abuse or of alcohol or drug abuse by one partner. Other types of pressures, including unemployment, financial difficulty, chronic illness, and even adapting to children, may create enormous STRESS on the marital relationship.

The Emotional Costs of Divorce Ending a marriage usually involves a period of emotional upheaval and painful readjustment. Each spouse may feel anger, guilt, loneliness, or a sense of rejection and failure. People involved in a divorce often experience grief or bereavement similar to that experienced after a death. Some formerly married people have so much trouble dealing with being single again that they persist in efforts to win the ex-partner back. Others jump into the first relationship that presents itself as a way of avoiding feelings of loneliness and failure. Most commonly, newly divorced people withdraw into themselves.

The divorce process may be so traumatic that one or both partners cannot handle it without help. Divorce counselors may be able to help the divorcing couple communicate more clearly and understand each other's needs and viewpoints. After the divorce, counselors may be useful in guiding the former partners to think about the future and what they have learned as a result of the marriage and divorce.

Children and Divorce The breakup of a marriage can have long-term negative effects on children. The children may feel guilty, angry, or abandoned. However, exposure to an unhappy or abusive marriage maintained solely for their sake may also hurt children. The impact of divorce on children is also made worse when the separated parents use their children as buffers or messengers, one parent relaying information through the children to the other parent. It is wise for children or adolescents who find themselves in this role to try to remove themselves from it and encourage their parents to communicate directly.

When divorcing parents share the same child-rearing values and when they can decide issues such as custody and visitation rights in a calm manner, the negative impact of the divorce on children can be greatly minimized. (See also MARRIAGE, 6; SPOUSE ABUSE, 8.)

DREAMS

Dreams are vivid, visual images that occur to people while they are sleeping. Most dreaming takes place during a stage of sleep called *REM* (rapid eye movement) *sleep*. In a normal night's sleep, a person experiences about four periods of REM sleep. People who do not get enough REM sleep over a period of time make up for it during succeeding nights. REM sleep (and presumably dreaming) seems to fill some physiological need; it has been found, for example, that laboratory animals that are deprived of REM sleep suffer strange effects, such as increased appetite for food

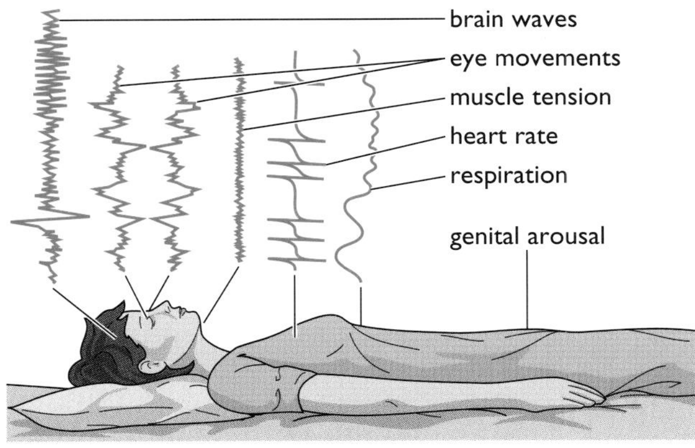

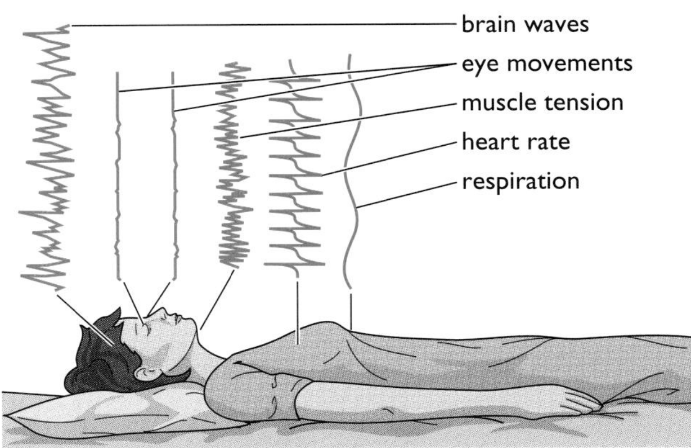

Effects of Dreams on the Body. *Dreams occur during REM sleep, when the body is inwardly very active but outwardly remains still.*

and sex. Dreams have also been considered to have psychological significance by Sigmund Freud and other psychoanalytic therapists.

Effects of Dreams on the Body During REM sleep, brain waves are rapid, heart rate rises, breathing is rapid and irregular, genitals may be aroused, and eyes move rapidly. At the same time, muscles are so relaxed that you do not move (see illustration: Effects of Dreams on the Body). Some researchers think that the rapid eye movements in REM sleep may indicate that you are watching your dream take place as if it were a movie or a real-life occurrence. Others believe that the movements indicate the operations of the nervous system.

The Nature of Dreams All dreams share some characteristics. The dreamer is always an active participant in the dream. Dreamers tend to forget dreams about ordinary events but remember ones that are fantastic or bizarre or involve strong emotional feelings. People are also inclined to remember dreams that occur shortly before they wake. Often dreams are disturbing, causing unpleasant or negative emotions such as anxiety, fear, and sadness. For example, many people have dreams about falling, about failing repeatedly at a task, or about being chased or attacked. Often stimuli received by the senses during sleep, such as a ringing phone, are incorporated into dreams. *Nightmares* are dreams that arouse very strong negative emotions, especially fright or terror.

Significance of Dreams Sigmund Freud, who developed the method of treating mental illness called psychoanalysis, advanced the first modern theory of the significance of dreams. He believed that dreams were harmless expressions of repressed desires, the fulfillment of wishes. He theorized that dreams were symbolic and that if they could be interpreted, they would provide information about the unconscious mind.

Many modern psychiatrists and psychologists have different ideas about the psychological meaning and usefulness of dreams. One theory is that dreams help people sort, reorganize, and fix in their memory some of the day's events. Any memories that are stored can come back in subsequent dreams. Other researchers believe that dreams are unresolved problems or emotional issues that the brain seeks to resolve during sleep.

Modern dream researchers have also looked at physiological reasons for dreams. One view is that dreams are the attempts of the higher brain (the cortex) to make sense out of random signals flowing from the brain stem; it does this by going through stored memories. Dreams may also provide the brain with the stimulation it needs to recharge and maintain the nervous system. (See also PSYCHIATRY; SLEEP PROBLEMS; SLEEP, **1**; SLEEP DISORDERS, **3**.)

Drug Therapy

Drug therapy is the use of chemicals to treat psychological disorders. Since the 1950s, drug therapy has been used to manage a range of abnormal behaviors either by correcting chemical imbalances in the nervous system or by relieving symptoms of psychological problems. Maintaining proper dosage and controlling unwanted side effects or reactions are two important factors psychiatrists and physicians consider when using drug therapy.

Types of Drug Therapy Psychiatric drugs are classified into three main categories (see chart: Drug Therapy). *Antianxiety drugs,* or *minor tranquilizers,* are used to treat ANXIETY DISORDERS. These drugs produce feelings of calmness by depressing the activity of the CENTRAL NERVOUS SYSTEM. *Antipsychotic drugs,* or *major tranquilizers,* are used to treat psychotic disorders such as SCHIZOPHRENIA. These drugs reduce symptoms of PSYCHOSIS, such as delusions and HALLUCINATIONS, and restore a more normal chemical balance in the brain. *Antidepressant drugs* are used to treat DEPRESSION. These drugs affect the chemical balance in the brain, causing the patient to feel more optimistic. Another type of mood-altering drug, the chemical lithium, is used to treat BIPOLAR DISORDER (manic-depressive illness). Although not technically an antidepressant, lithium stabilizes the mood swings that are characteristic of this disorder.

Benefits and Costs Drug therapy is normally used in conjunction with some form of PSYCHOTHERAPY. Although psychiatric medications do not cure mental disorders in the usual sense, they help control the expression of symptoms so that quality of life can be improved and therapy can be more productive. Ironically, the effectiveness of these drugs can

DRUG THERAPY

Type of drug	Generic name	Brand name
Antianxiety drugs (minor tranquilizers)	Chlordiazepoxide Diazepam	Librium Valium
Antipsychotic drugs (major tranquilizers)	Chlorpromazine Haloperidol	Thorazine Haldol
Antidepressant drugs	Imipramine	Tofranil
	Amitriptyline	Elavil
	Lithium	Eskalith
	Fluoxetine hydrochloride	Prozac

be a problem, in that patients sometimes feel cured, stop taking their medication, and need to be readmitted to an institution.

The use of psychiatric drugs has other drawbacks as well. Side effects can be severe, especially with antipsychotic drugs. Antianxiety drugs, which are very widely prescribed, can be addictive if improperly used. Patients can develop a *tolerance* to a drug, which means that more of the drug is necessary to achieve the desired effect. A physical *dependence* can also develop, making the eventual withdrawal a painful experience. In addition, *overdosing* on a drug is a danger if the patient is taking other drugs that suppress the central nervous system or using alcohol. (See also MENTAL ILLNESS; ADDICTION, 7; ANTIDEPRESSANTS, 7; SEDATIVES, 7; TOLERANCE, 7.)

DYING AND BEREAVEMENT

Dying and death are the last phases of human life. The way a person deals with dying and death is shaped by a number of factors, such as personality and age. *Bereavement* is the process of grieving for the loss of a loved friend or family member. The relationship of the bereaved to the person who has died is the major factor in determining the intensity of emotion during bereavement. Although expressions of sadness and grief are individual to each person, both dying and bereavement have been described as periods during which people experience a series of reactions as they try to cope with the sorrow of these events.

Stages of Dying In 1969, psychiatrist Elisabeth Kübler-Ross proposed that people who know they are dying pass through five progressive emotional stages. According to Kübler-Ross, who based her findings on interviews with elderly, terminally ill people, the first stage is *denial* of death, followed by a period of *anger* or a feeling of "why me?" Next, there is an attempt to postpone death, perhaps by *bargaining* with doctors, family members, or God. The next stage is *depression,* followed finally by peaceful *acceptance* of death.

The Kübler-Ross model has been very influential among medical and helping professionals in the way they respond to the emotions of terminally ill people. Since the model was first proposed, however, researchers have found little evidence that dying people necessarily pass through all these stages. Some people move back and forth between stages until achieving a resolution. There appears to be considerable variability in the way people approach death and dying.

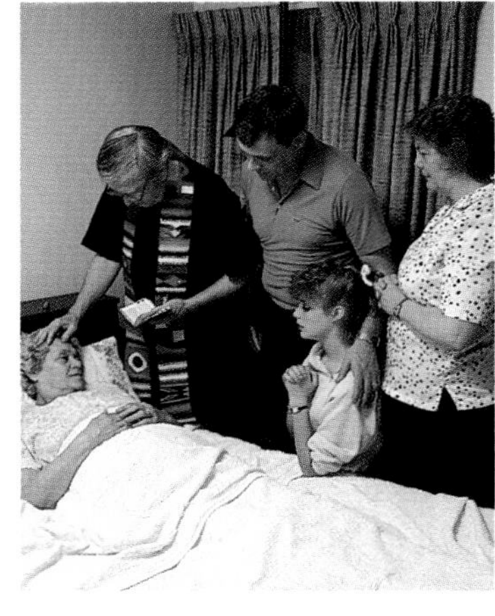

Dying and Bereavement. *Dying and bereavement are inevitable parts of life. Facing death and loss provokes different emotional reactions in different people.*

Stages of Bereavement The grief that follows the loss of a loved one has also been described in terms of progressive stages. At first there may be a sense of *numbness,* lasting from several days to several months, when the bereaved person seems dazed or shocked. The reality of death does not seem to be fully realized during this period, and there may even be denial of the death. HALLUCINATIONS, in which a bereaved person senses that he or she has seen or heard the dead person, are common experiences. After the numbness wears off, the full realization of the death occurs. Feelings of ANXIETY, ANGER, guilt, resentment, and despair are common and may lead to DEPRESSION. Gradual *acceptance* of and adjustment to the loss then begins, and the bereaved person may start to make positive plans for the future and build a new identity that is separate from the person who has died.

Although acceptance usually occurs within 2 years, many people, especially those who experience the sudden death of a loved one, may still be in a state of depression and have unresolved feelings of grief for as long as 4 to 7 years after the loss.

Other types of loss besides those involving death can also result in many of the feelings of bereavement. Grieving can occur following such events as the loss of a parent through divorce, the loss of a friend who has moved, the loss of a boyfriend or girlfriend through breaking up, or the loss of a prized role, such as a seat in student government.

Coping with Dying and Bereavement Family and friends can provide important support during dying and bereavement. Comforting someone who is facing death may involve helping that person make a positive review of his or her life and accomplishments. For a bereaved person, family and friends can provide reassurance and encourage the person to express his or her emotions. Special counseling or psychotherapy may be helpful during periods of depression or apathy.

HEALTHY CHOICES

The following strategies may help a bereaved person cope with the loss of a loved one: Allow grief to happen and accept comfort from others; do not be in a hurry to make major life changes or to eliminate reminders of the departed; try to replace negative thoughts with more positive ones; ward off depression by engaging in useful activities; and join a support group to share feelings with others who have faced a similar loss. (See also DEATH, **1.**)

DYSLEXIA

see LEARNING DISABILITY

ELECTROCONVULSIVE THERAPY

Electroconvulsive therapy (ECT), also known as shock therapy, is used primarily to treat people with severe DEPRESSION. In ECT, electrodes are placed on one or both sides of the patient's head, and an electric current is passed into the brain, causing a convulsion (see illustration: Electroconvulsive Therapy). The therapy usually consists of a series of treatments spaced over a period of several weeks. ECT causes little discomfort to the patient, who receives an anesthetic and a muscle relaxant before treatment. However, there are potential complications, including temporary confusion and amnesia. Memory of the immediate period around ECT may be lost permanently.

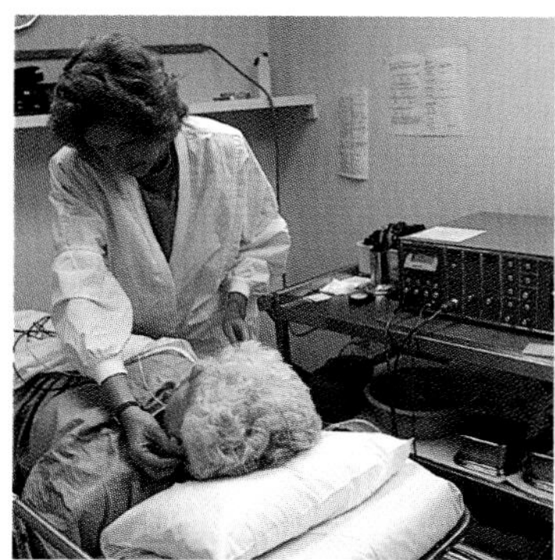

Electroconvulsive Therapy. *This type of therapy is an effective way to treat patients with severe depression, but it remains controversial.*

ECT can be an effective therapy, but its use is controversial. During the early years of its use, patients sometimes had severe injuries, such as broken bones, as a result of the strong convulsion. Today, with advances in knowledge and technology, such side effects are usually minimal. Nevertheless, many people are still wary of ECT, in part because no one can explain how it works. Generally, it is a treatment of last resort for severely depressed patients who have not responded to DRUG THERAPY.

Emotion

Emotion refers to how people feel about and react to the events and relationships in their lives. An emotion is a very complex experience involving both psychological and physical processes. Pleasant emotions, such as HAPPINESS and LOVE, are termed *positive emotions;* other generally unpleasant emotions, including ANGER and FEAR, are termed *negative emotions.* Most people experience a wide variety of both positive and negative emotions every day.

Emotions enrich people's lives and influence their behavior. People take actions that arouse positive emotions and avoid negative ones. Charles Darwin, the great naturalist, theorized that emotions evolved because they helped humans survive. Fear and anger, for example, help humans cope with threatening situations; happiness and love help people form bonds with one another that increase their chances of surviving.

The Components of Emotion Emotions can be broken down into four components: subjective, cognitive, physiological, and behavioral. The *subjective* component is the feeling itself, pleasant or unpleasant, faint or strong. The *cognitive* aspect includes the thoughts, beliefs, and knowledge that help shape the emotions of each individual. For example, the knowledge that a close friend is moving away can make a person feel sad.

Events that arouse emotions trigger many physiological changes. When a person experiences fear, for example, the heart rate increases and the pupils of the eyes dilate.

Events that arouse emotions trigger many *physiological* changes. When a person experiences fear, for example, the heart rate increases, breathing becomes deeper and more rapid, the pupils of the eyes dilate, and the sweat glands increase their output. These physical changes are often called the *fight-or-flight response* because they prepare a person to confront or flee from danger. This involuntary physical response arises from the *sympathetic nervous system,* the part of the AUTONOMIC NERVOUS SYSTEM that readies the body for emergency. Most emotions, both positive and negative, trigger similar physical changes. Joy, for example, can speed up the heart rate, and anger can increase blood pressure.

The fourth component of emotions, the *behavioral,* consists of the outward expressions of an emotion—the gestures, posture, and tone of voice that someone assumes in expressing an emotion. Researchers have discovered that certain emotions, such as happiness, anger, and surprise, cause the face to assume expressions that are virtually the same the world over.

Theories of Emotion No one knows exactly how emotions arise, but several theories have been advanced during the past 100 years. According to the *James-Lange theory,* first proposed in the late nineteenth century, emotional feelings are triggered by the body's physiological reactions to an emotion-arousing event. In other words, people feel happiness because they laugh rather than laugh because they are happy (see chart: Theories of Emotion).

Another theory was proposed by psychologists Walter Cannon and Philip Bard in the 1920s and 1930s. The *Cannon-Bard theory* holds that emotion-arousing situations stimulate a part of the brain called the thalamus, which then relays signals simultaneously to emotion centers in the cerebral cortex and to the autonomic nervous system. Later researchers determined that the relay center for emotional and physical arousal is probably in the hypothalamus and not the thalamus. (See also BRAIN, **1**.)

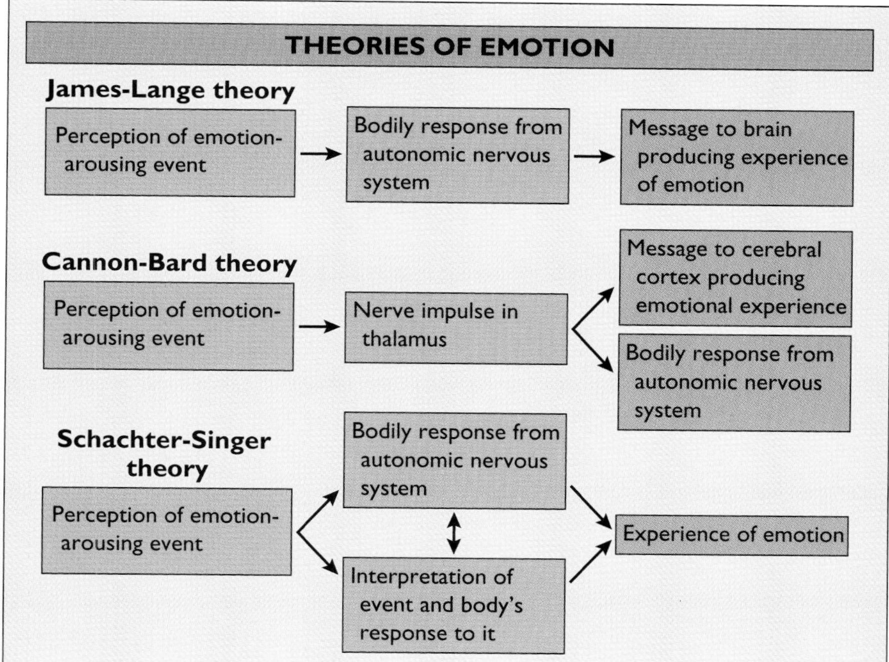

Theories of Emotion. *In the James-Lange theory, emotions occur after the body is aroused. The Cannon-Bard theory proposes that emotions and arousal occur at the same time. The Schachter-Singer or cognitive labeling theory suggests that arousal in the body causes the brain to determine a reason for the arousal; the emotion occurs once the brain has interpreted the arousal.*

A third theory, the Schachter-Singer or *cognitive labeling theory,* explains emotions as a combination of a physiological response and an interpretation of that response based on knowledge of the situation. Someone crying at a funeral, for example, would usually interpret his or her emotion as sadness, whereas someone crying at a wedding might perceive it as happiness.

The Development of Emotions Emotions are a complex combination of genetic factors, culture, and upbringing. Some researchers believe that the development of emotions follows a biological timetable. Certain basic emotions, such as pleasure and distress, seem to be present at birth. At 12 months, a child has usually developed all of the *primary emotions*—surprise, fear, anger, disgust, sadness, and happiness. The more complex *secondary emotions,* including embarrassment, shame, guilt, pride, and jealousy, generally develop later, between the ages of 2 and 6. (See also DEVELOPMENTAL PSYCHOLOGY.)

Secondary emotions are sometimes thought of as mixtures of primary emotions. Jealousy, for example, reflects both love and fear, the fear of losing a partner in a close relationship. Sigmund Freud, the founder of psychoanalysis, explained emotions such as shame and guilt in terms of the development of a person's conscience (which he called the *superego*). Guilt, he said, is a feeling of remorse that occurs when a person violates his or her personal code of ethics or responsibilities.

An individual's upbringing and culture have a profound influence on the development and expression of emotions. In some cultures, children may be taught to express certain emotions, such as pride or affection, while in others they may be encouraged to suppress expression of these emotions.

Emotions and Health Emotions can greatly affect a person's health. People who experience strong negative emotions over a period of time can be emotionally disabled. For example, DEPRESSION is a deep, prolonged feeling of sadness that can cause people to lose all interest in life.

The relationship between emotions and physical illness is more complex. The arousal of strong emotions is often associated with STRESS, the body's response to conflicts and changes and a contributing factor in many illnesses. Chronic stress sometimes produces PSYCHOSOMATIC DISORDERS, which are physical illnesses that result primarily from emotional rather than physiological causes. Stress and emotions may also affect the body's immune system. Prolonged negative stress associated with negative emotions can weaken the immune system and lessen its ability to fight off diseases. By the same token, positive emotions and laughter may have a beneficial effect on health. Conversely, physical illness may cause fear, anxiety, or depression, which may interfere with treatment and recovery. The study of the complex relationship between emotions, stress, and the body's immune system is one concern of the relatively new field of HEALTH PSYCHOLOGY. (See also IMMUNE SYSTEM, **1**.)

FAMILY

A family is made up of two or more individuals who live together in one household. Family members are usually, but not always, related by blood, marriage, or adoption. Family relationships provide an individual's first social network. Families also provide the setting in which children learn VALUES and patterns of behavior that can last a lifetime.

Types of Families In America today, families are increasingly varied. Four basic types are most common:

- The *nuclear family* is the traditional model, a family group made up of a couple and their child or children living in their own household.
- A *blended family* is a family that combines after divorced or widowed parents remarry. It includes stepbrothers or stepsisters who live with parents in a single household.
- A *single-parent family* is headed by one parent, more often by a mother but sometimes by a father.
- An *extended family* includes in one household the nuclear family plus other relatives such as grandparents, uncles, aunts, or cousins.

> Blended families, which now account for one in every six American families, must adjust to many situations not faced by nuclear families.

Challenges for Families Each of the different types of family groupings faces its own particular challenges. Blended families, which now account for one in every six American families, must adjust to many situations not faced by nuclear families. Problems can arise because of conflicting ideas about authority, family relationships, and traditions. However, studies show that the overall emotional, social, and family adjustment of people in blended families and those in nuclear families is not very different.

Single-parent families result from the death of a spouse, from divorce or desertion, or from the decision of some women to have children without marrying. More than 20 percent of American children now live

Extended Families. *Extended families may contain three generations living in the same household.*

in families headed by a single mother. Single-parent families generally face more stress than do families with two parents. Problems can occur because incomes are generally low (currently half of all single mothers live below the poverty line) and because fulfilling the responsibilities of work and child care is more difficult without the support of a partner. For these reasons, single parents often need help and support from family members, friends, and the community.

Extended families face the challenge of meeting individual needs for the privacy and independence of the adults in the household. If lines of authority are not clear-cut and consistent, children may face the conflict of having to answer to several adults in addition to their parents.

RISK FACTORS

The Importance of the Family The family plays a crucial role in a child's development. *Dysfunctional families* are those in which members relate to each other in unhealthy and damaging ways, including lack of caring, poor communication, and denial of or inability to cope with problems. In many cases, parental abuse of alcohol or drugs leads to patterns of dysfunction. Neglect and abuse may be part of a child's experience in a dysfunctional family. Such families can have a lasting negative effect on the way individuals see themselves and others. Stable, fully functioning families, on the other hand, provide children with the love, care, support, and encouragement to grow to be healthy, well-adjusted adults. (See also DIVORCE; CHILD ABUSE, 8.)

FEAR

Fear is an intense, unpleasant EMOTION that people experience when confronted by dangers or by situations or objects that represent danger. Depending on the circumstances, the fear response may be necessary for health and survival or detrimental to well-being. For instance, fear motivates people to flee from physical danger, and fear of punishment or other negative results may encourage people to do what is expected of them rather than act in an unacceptable way. On the other hand, fear can

Bravery. *These firefighters demonstrate bravery as they face danger in order to put out a fire.*

be paralyzing, prompting confusion and preventing appropriate action from taking place.

Fear causes a physiological reaction as the body prepares to escape from or face a danger. The heart beats faster, blood pressure rises, muscles tense, and breathing accelerates. If the fear lasts a long time, the physiological response can have negative effects on the body, becoming a chronic stressor. (See also STRESS.)

When a danger is real, an appropriate level of fear is a normal, healthy response. Some people, however, become incapacitated by excessive fears that arise in response to imaginary threats. These individuals may need PSYCHOTHERAPY or DRUG THERAPY to overcome their irrational fears, especially if the fears interfere with daily life (such as *phobias* and other ANXIETY DISORDERS). On the other hand, some people demonstrate *fearlessness,* or an apparent lack of fear. Fearlessness is not the same as *bravery,* which is overcoming personal fears to achieve a worthwhile goal. True fearlessness can cause people to behave recklessly in the face of real danger or to engage in frivolously dangerous activities, such as Russian roulette. Fearlessness can also be expressed by criminals who show no fear of the consequences of their acts.

Psychologists believe that although some fears are instinctive, most are learned. Infants, for instance, are born with a fear of falling and a fear of loud noises. Different fears then develop as children get older. Many childhood fears, such as fear of the dark and fear of strangers, are usually outgrown. As thinking skills increase throughout adolescence and adulthood, people may develop different fears, such as fear of failure or fear of rejection. Learning skills that give you a sense of competence and social capability can help decrease such fears.

FRIENDSHIP

HEALTHY CHOICES

Friendship is a close attachment between people who feel affection and esteem for each other. The desire for friendship springs from the basic human needs to belong and to LOVE and be loved. With friends, people can share recreational activities, intellectual pursuits, and personal celebrations. Individuals turn to friends for advice, assistance, and empathy (understanding) and affection. They rely on friends for emotional support to help them through difficult experiences. Friendships are RELATIONSHIPS that contribute to both HAPPINESS and health.

The Nature of Friendship During early childhood, friendships form among children who play together. Friendships deepen and become more complex as a child matures, but it is not until adolescence that INTIMACY becomes an essential part of friendship.

Finding and keeping friends means making a commitment to be sensitive to another's needs and preferences. It means taking an emotional risk to share deeper feelings and establish intimacy. A friendship needs time to develop, as well as tolerance and humor on both sides.

Why People Form Friendships Psychologists believe that several factors help determine whether a new acquaintance becomes a friend. Two of the most influential factors are proximity and similarity. People who

Making New Friends. *A shared interest often leads to new friendships.*

live or work *in proximity,* or close to one another, often become friends. In addition, these people usually have many *similarities*—they may share ethnic backgrounds, socioeconomic status, or attitudes. Similarity is a powerful influence on friendship because people tend to prefer to be around those who are most like them and share their background and interests. On the other hand, psychologists also point out that some people form friendships not because of similarity but because the other person has qualities they lack; a shy person and an outgoing person, then, may become friends because they complement each other. For such a friendship to flourish, however, the individual traits must generally be compatible, or able to coexist without causing too much conflict.

Physical attractiveness is also a factor that may have an impact on the formation of friendships, especially at the beginning. Attractiveness often loses its importance, however, once a friendship develops. Also, the perception of attractiveness may increase as a relationship develops.

Friendships and Health Recent studies of people with heart ailments and elderly people suggest that friendship strongly influences health. Heart patients without a spouse or close friends were three times more likely to die within 5 years of diagnosis than patients who were married or had a close friend. Another study of healthy older people found that those with close friendships generally had a greater ability to fight disease and lower levels of such substances as cholesterol in the blood than had those without close relationships.

Friendships can also help people manage the effects of STRESS. Unfortunately, people who lead busy lives or who are bothered by fears and concerns often have little time or energy to form and maintain friendships. These relationships, however, are important for maintaining health and add to the joy in living. (See also COMMUNICATION; RESPONSIBILITY; SOCIAL SKILLS.)

GUILT

see EMOTION

Hallucination

A hallucination is a sensation or perception that has no external source. It involves seeing, hearing, feeling, tasting, or smelling something that is not really there. People sometimes have hallucinations during periods of overwhelming grief, fatigue, or STRESS. However, vivid hallucinations that occur frequently may be due to serious physical or mental disorders, the heavy use of alcohol or drugs, or withdrawal from alcohol or drug addiction.

RISK FACTORS

Hallucinations are a major characteristic of SCHIZOPHRENIA, a serious form of mental illness. The hallucinations of people with schizophrenia are uncontrollable, very intense, and may occur repeatedly. They often include voices, which may be insulting, threatening, or commanding. Schizophrenic hallucinations may involve the other senses as well—visions of imagined people or objects, for example, or imagined sensations in the body or on the skin.

RISK FACTORS

The use of *hallucinogens,* such as the drugs LSD and PCP, often cause visual hallucinations. These visions may progress from patterns of geometric shapes to more complex scenes and images. The hallucinations usually occur while the drug is active in the body, although they can reappear spontaneously long afterward, especially in people who have taken heavy doses of the drug over a period of time.

Vivid visual hallucinations are also characteristic of *delirium,* a mental disturbance that can result from physical illness or withdrawal from alcohol addiction. (See also DELIRIUM TREMENS, 7; HALLUCINOGENS, 7; WITHDRAWAL SYNDROME, 7.)

Happiness

Happiness is a long-lasting, positive emotional state that people experience when they are generally satisfied with their lives and take pleasure in everyday activities. Happiness is a combination of *contentment,* a feeling of satisfaction with things as they are, and *joy,* a positive EMOTION resulting from pleasurable activities. Many different elements are involved in a person's happiness.

Happiness. *A satisfying family life and close friendships contribute enormously to happiness.*

What Makes People Happy Researchers have identified several basic characteristics that contribute to happiness. Studies have shown that happy people tend to have high SELF-ESTEEM and compare themselves favorably to other people in similar situations. Unhappy people, however, tend to compare themselves unfavorably to others. Psychologists have also found that an individual's PERSONALITY plays a significant role in whether or not that person is happy. People who are warm, outgoing, and involved with other people tend to be happier than people with negative traits such as hostility, ANXIETY, or guilt. In addition, the particular circumstances of a person's life have an effect on happiness. People who are in LOVE, who are able to meet their life goals, and who have had good RELATIONSHIPS with FAMILY and friends tend to enjoy a high level of happiness.

People can take some steps to become happier. They can begin by trying to have a more positive outlook on life. Setting realistic goals to work toward can contribute to a person's happiness, as can involvement

HEALTHY CHOICES

in activities that provide short-term pleasures. Finally, making efforts to improve relationships with family and close friends seems worthwhile because satisfying relationships play a key role in personal happiness.

Health Psychology

Health psychology is the study of the relationship between PSYCHOLOGY and physical health, with an emphasis on wellness and the prevention of illness. Health psychologists study how health is affected by people's emotions, personalities, lifestyles, and behavior. They are concerned with the promotion and maintenance of good health and with helping people eliminate behaviors that are harmful to physical health—such as smoking—and establish beneficial behaviors—such as exercise. Some health psychologists are engaged in research, while others work directly with patients or the general public.

Health Psychologists. *Health psychologists help people understand how emotions, lifestyles, and behavior affect health.*

Health psychology is a relatively new field. The influence of the mind and behavior on physical health has been recognized since ancient times, but the understanding of medicine and human behavior was not sufficient for the scientific practice of health psychology. The emphasis in medical research through much of the twentieth century had been on discovering and treating the physiological causes of disease, while virtually ignoring psychological factors. Since the 1970s, however, health psychology has begun to gain much attention in medical research and practice.

The underlying assumption of health psychology is that behavior and other psychological factors play a significant role in the development of many illnesses. Health psychologists work with physicians and other health professionals in an effort to determine how psychological factors contribute to health problems or how these factors may be used in treatment and prevention. One area of research is in the relationship between STRESS and illness; researchers have found evidence that stress plays a role in a number of diseases, including cancer and heart disease. Health psychologists are also studying the effects of stress on people undergoing medical treatment and on those with a chronic health problem. Other areas of research in health psychology include pain management and ways of encouraging patients to follow medical advice and prescribed lifestyle changes. (See also BEHAVIOR MODIFICATION; PSYCHOSOMATIC DISORDERS; SLEEP PROBLEMS.)

Heredity and Environment

Heredity and environment are the two key factors that determine how an individual develops. Your *heredity* consists of certain characteristics that your parents passed on to you through their genes. Your *environment* consists of the elements that surround and influence your development, such as the place where you live, your FAMILY, peer group, and ethnic background.

Psychologists have long debated the significance of heredity and environment on human development. This "nature versus nurture" debate questions whether heredity (nature) has more influence than has

The Influence of Environment. *Identical twins, formed when a single fertilized egg divides in two, have the same genetic makeup. Studying identical twins that were adopted after birth into different families can help researchers assess the relative influence of heredity and environment on personality.*

environment (nurture). Most experts now agree that the differences among individuals can be explained only by considering both hereditary and environmental factors.

Hereditary Factors Found in every cell in the body, *genes* contain the chemical blueprints that help determine an individual's physical and mental traits. Genes affect human development in several ways: They influence physical characteristics (such as height and eye color), the rate of physical maturation, mental ability, and numerous personality *traits* and tendencies. Many psychologists believe that heredity provides a particular range of possibilities for each person but that environment shapes and modifies these possibilities to create the specific characteristics of an individual.

Environmental Factors The impact of environment on human development can be significant. Researchers have found that infants who live in environments where they are deprived of social and emotional stimulation fail to achieve the potential physical growth indicated by their heredity. By the same token, when the environmental stimulation of children is increased, their development appears to be enhanced.

The interaction of environment and heredity continues throughout a person's life. What people eat and drink, the knowledge they gain and use, and the RELATIONSHIPS they experience all can and do affect the expression of hereditary traits. (See also GENETICS, **6**.)

HYPERACTIVITY

Hyperactivity is a form of behavior that is marked by extreme restlessness and overactivity. In children, this behavior is often associated with LEARNING DISABILITIES and attention deficit disorder, an inability to pay attention for longer than a few minutes. The association of hyperactivity with attentional problems is so great that the condition is called *attention deficit hyperactivity disorder* (ADHD). There is no known cause or cure for ADHD, but various therapies can help control hyperactive and inattentive behavior and improve achievement in school.

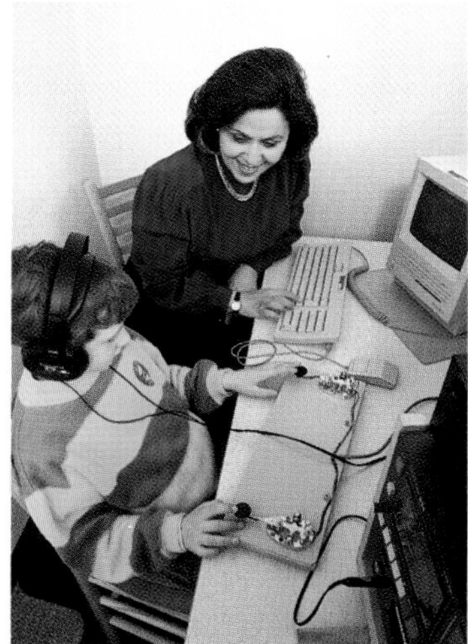

Computer Therapy. *Children with ADHD are often attentive and learn well with computers because the frequent feedback keeps them engaged and focused on the task.*

Children with ADHD have difficulty concentrating and behaving appropriately in school. They tend to be impatient and easily distracted and have trouble organizing their work, sitting quietly, and waiting to be recognized before speaking. Children with ADHD may also have difficulty establishing social relationships because they may be seen as disruptive or out of control by adults and other children.

Treatment Physicians often prescribe a stimulant drug such as ritalin to treat hyperactivity; the use of stimulants seems to improve the child's ability to maintain attention and concentration. Yet the use of these drugs is controversial. Without therapy to teach behavioral self-control and social skills, the drugs merely control symptoms. In addition, they can cause adverse side effects such as insomnia and loss of appetite. However, appropriate use of ritalin and other drugs can reduce STRESS for the child, family, and teachers, because the child can obey rules, is less active, and has a greater opportunity to please adults.

Many hyperactive children are also treated with a form of PSYCHOTHERAPY called *behavioral therapy* to develop self-control and social skills. Behavioral therapy incorporates frequent, immediate feedback to behavior, including rewarding appropriate behavior until inappropriate behavior gradually disappears. Children with ADHD may require special teaching techniques or supplemental learning activities in a regular classroom.

In the 1970s and early 1980s, some researchers believed that hyperactivity was linked to eating too much sugar or to certain foods and food additives. One such researcher, Dr. Benjamin Feingold, devised a diet free of these substances, which he believed could cure or control hyperactivity. Recent research now indicates that such a diet has little effect on hyperactive children. (See also RITALIN, 7.)

HYPNOSIS

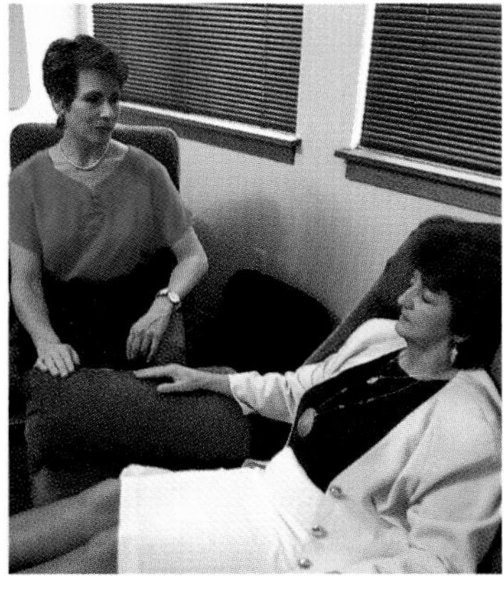

Hypnosis. *The ability of a person to be hypnotized depends on the person's personality, motivation, and imagination and on the amount of trust the individual has in the hypnotist.*

Hypnosis is a temporary state of deep relaxation that a person enters willingly, usually with the help of another person. People under hypnosis readily accept the suggestions of the person who hypnotized them. This can result in a change in behavior and perceptions and in the recollection of forgotten memories. Hypnosis was first practiced in the eighteenth century by the German physician Franz Anton Mesmer (hence the term *mesmerized*).

The use of hypnosis as a medical and psychological treatment method has been questioned and debated. It has, however, been used successfully to relieve pain and to help people stop addictive behavior such as smoking and overeating. Some psychotherapists employ hypnosis to help clients reduce ANXIETY or to remember unpleasant information that they cannot recall consciously.

How Hypnosis Is Induced A hypnotist induces the hypnotic state by asking a person to concentrate on an object and by suggesting that the person is feeling relaxed and sleepy. While hypnotized, people comprehend and accept a hypnotist's instruction. Under hypnosis, people will not usually do what they believe to be harmful or immoral.

A hypnotist who is helping someone overcome an addictive habit such as smoking may give an instruction about modifying behavior while the person is under hypnosis. In some cases, this *posthypnotic suggestion* will cause a change in behavior even though the person may be unaware of the instruction. Posthypnotic suggestions are also used to treat a variety of health problems including SLEEP PROBLEMS and compulsive overeating. (See also MIND; PSYCHOTHERAPY.)

HYPOCHONDRIA

Hypochondria is an ongoing, overwhelming preoccupation with illness. A person with hypochondria worries constantly that he or she has a serious disease, although no physical disorder can be found to account for the symptoms. This person may interpret a minor physical symptom—a headache, for example—as a sign of a fatal condition—a brain tumor. Or he or she may focus on a certain organ, such as the heart, and worry that it is affected by a serious disorder. People with hypochondria genuinely believe that they are ill and often assume that physicians are failing to diagnose their illness. Typically, they visit many doctors and are disappointed to hear that nothing is wrong.

The causes of hypochondria are not fully understood, but it often accompanies other psychological disorders, such as ANXIETY DISORDERS. One theory suggests that people with hypochondria may focus on and describe physical symptoms instead of expressing emotional pain. PSYCHOTHERAPY can be helpful in identifying and resolving the conflicts or disorders that underlie hypochondria. (See also PSYCHOSOMATIC DISORDERS.)

Hypochondria. *People with hypochondria worry constantly and excessively about their physical health.*

HYSTERIA

Hysteria is an outdated term that was used to describe a range of physical or mental symptoms that had no identifiable physical cause. Taken from the Greek word for "uterus," *hysteria* was originally used to describe overly emotional or dramatic behaviors that were believed to affect women only. Today, psychologists have replaced the term *hysteria* with more specific diagnostic descriptions, such as *somatoform disorders.*

The term *mass hysteria* is currently used to describe an uncontrollable outburst of fear that spreads from person to person. Mass hysteria includes group obsessions such as the Salem witch-hunts in seventeenth-century colonial Massachusetts and the U.S. Senate hearings held to uncover Communists in the 1950s. (See also NEUROSIS; PSYCHOSOMATIC DISORDERS.)

INTELLIGENCE

Intelligence is not easily defined or measured because it includes human qualities and abilities that are not directly observable. It is an important concept, however, because these qualities and abilities can affect how well an individual copes with and adapts to his or her environment.

Definitions of Intelligence Experts have developed several different definitions of intelligence. Some define intelligence as a single factor—an ability to reason, make judgments, solve problems, and engage in types of thinking that result in some type of LEARNING. Others believe that intelligence consists of several distinct mental abilities, such as verbal ability, memory, mathematical ability, and so on. Still others define intelligence as mental functions that provide individuals with adaptability, which enables them to cope with, adapt to, and modify their environments. A definition used by many psychologists incorporates several of these ideas. They define intelligence as the capacity to solve different

IQ Testing. *Standard IQ tests are not necessarily good measures of overall intelligence, but they are good predictors of an individual's ability to succeed in school.*

types of problems and adapt to a changing environment by applying knowledge to new situations.

Testing Intelligence There is no absolute way to measure all the diverse intellectual abilities of an individual. The most any intelligence test can do is to measure certain abilities that may be useful in particular situations, such as in school. The purpose of intelligence tests, or *IQ tests,* is to measure such mental abilities as verbal and mathematical skills and the ability to understand directions and to recognize objects. (The name *IQ* comes from the way these tests were originally scored, which gave the result as an intelligence quotient.)

Standard IQ tests are not necessarily good measurements of overall intelligence or competence in such areas as musical ability or athletic skill. Nor do they indicate absolutely a person's ability to learn. One problem with many intelligence tests is that they are culturally biased, meaning that the questions will be more familiar to certain cultural or ethnic groups than to others. Despite their limitations, IQ tests remain the primary means of assessing certain skills and mental abilities. They are good predictors of an individual's ability to succeed in school.

Differences in Intelligence Individuals, of course, do differ in their ability to solve problems, learn and use information, and cope with their environments. One of the most controversial issues concerning intelligence is whether these individual differences are due primarily to genetic, or hereditary, factors or to environmental (family upbringing, culture, and so on) ones. Most experts agree that both genetic and environmental factors play a part in determining intelligence. They believe that genetic factors set upper and lower limits on an individual's intellectual capacity but that environmental factors affect whether the individual will reach his or her potential. (See also HEREDITY AND ENVIRONMENT.)

INTIMACY

Emotional Intimacy. *People can be emotionally intimate without being sexually involved. By the same token, people can be sexually intimate without emotional intimacy.*

Emotional intimacy is the sharing of personal feelings, thoughts, and experiences in a relationship between two people. People who are intimate tend to value one another and to give and receive understanding. The need for intimacy is personal; some people require more than others.

Intimacy is an important part of close RELATIONSHIPS, especially those involving LOVE. Friends, romantic partners, and parents and their children often have intimate relationships. Intimate relationships change as people grow, but the need for intimacy remains strong throughout life.

People who are able to establish intimacy in their relationships usually have certain traits. They generally have a positive SELF-IMAGE, the ability to trust, the capacity to express and share EMOTIONS, and a commitment to the other person in the relationship. In addition, they probably enjoyed close relationships as they were growing up.

People who lack intimate relationships may feel lonely and depressed. These feelings sometimes lead to serious problems such as alcoholism, drug abuse, and SUICIDE.

IQ

see INTELLIGENCE

Jealousy

see EMOTION

Leadership

Leadership is the process through which an individual uses influence or persuasion to guide and motivate others to attain goals. Leaders acquire influence in several ways. Some attain it through their strong emotional appeal, or *charisma.* Others attain influence because of their expertise and knowledge. Still others become leaders because they have power to reward or punish.

Leadership Qualities Leaders often possess such characteristics as intelligence, self-confidence, an energetic nature, and an outgoing personality. Circumstances, however, are also an important factor in determining leadership, and different situations may call for different types of leaders. A conflict situation requires a leader who is good at soothing people and working out disputes. A complex project needs a leader with planning and organizational abilities. In some cases, leadership is shared by two or more people.

Types of Leaders Not all leaders act the same way. *Authoritarian leaders* do not share power but instead give orders and make all decisions themselves. *Democratic leaders* share authority and try to involve others in making decisions. *Laissez-faire* (leh say FAIR) *leaders* serve primarily as a resource for others; group members have decision-making power as well as authority. The appropriateness of each of these styles of leadership depends on the circumstances and needs of the particular group.

Charismatic Leadership. *President John F. Kennedy was a charismatic leader; he evoked strong emotions in the people who supported him.*

Learning

Learning can be defined as a relatively permanent change in behavior or knowledge that occurs as a result of experience. Learning is an essential part of human behavior and is part of nearly every aspect of life at all ages. Psychologists recognize several basic types of learning, including CONDITIONING, modeling, and cognitive learning.

Conditioning Conditioning, which is also called associative learning, occurs when a person makes an association or connection between a stimulus (event, person, or object) and a response (behavior). In *classical conditioning,* a person learns to associate an involuntary, or automatic, response such as an emotion or a physical reflex action with a particular stimulus. For example, a person who becomes violently ill after eating fish may associate illness with fish and will start to feel nauseated whenever he or she is given fish to eat. If a singer is embarrassed by forgetting the words to a song during a performance, he or she may blush with embarrassment when hearing the song again. A response acquired this way can be changed by learning a new association between a stimulus and response.

With operant conditioning, the consequences of a person's behavior influence whether or not the person will act in the same way in the future.

With a second type of conditioning called *operant conditioning,* the consequences of a person's behavior influence whether or not the person will act (or operate) in the same way in the future. For example, when a child crying in pain is comforted by a parent, the child learns that he or she will get attention by crying. At a later time, the child wanting attention may cry just to be noticed. With this type of conditioning (also called instrumental conditioning), people make a voluntary, or intentional, response to a stimulus. When they see that the response has a favorable result, they are likely to act in the same way again. For example, if an employee who works hard receives a raise, the person is likely to continue working hard in the hope of additional raises.

An important aspect of operant conditioning is *reinforcement*—response to an action that increases the likelihood of a desired behavior being repeated. Reinforcement can take many forms, such as food, money, special privileges, and the approval of others. Reinforcement may be either positive or negative, with positive reinforcement being the more effective. Positive reinforcement is a pleasant stimulus, such as the salary increase mentioned earlier, that strengthens the probability of a behavior recurring when the stimulus is applied. Negative reinforcement is a disagreeable stimulus that, when removed, strengthens the probability of a behavior recurring. For example, a student studies to avoid a failing grade. Negative reinforcement is different from punishment because a disagreeable stimulus is removed following an appropriate behavior rather than applied after an inappropriate behavior. A student who doesn't study and fails a test may be punished by having the car keys taken away.

Modeling Modeling, which involves imitating the behaviors of others, is another important type of learning. Individuals often learn how to behave in a situation by watching others and then behaving in the same way. This is especially true of young children who often try to copy the actions of their brothers or sisters, parents, and other adults.

Reinforcement and Practice. *Reinforcement is an important part of the learning process. Positive reinforcement (above left), such as an award and the approval of others, encourages a person to continue the behavior that earned the award. Psychologists have found that practice (above right), which is a factor affecting learning, is more effective when spread out and interspersed with rest periods rather than done nonstop.*

In modeling, individuals can learn to perform certain actions or to avoid them. (See also ROLE MODEL.)

Cognitive Learning Cognitive learning involves the formation of mental abstractions such as CONCEPTS, theories, and generalizations, which help organize the world and make it more understandable.

People are not born with these mental abstractions. They must be learned over time, and many psychologists recognize distinct stages of cognitive development during which only certain thought processes are possible. For example, the psychologist Jean Piaget (pyah ZHAY) established a series of five stages of cognitive development from birth through adulthood. An individual's progression through these stages depends on physical and mental development and on life experiences. During all stages, cognitive learning occurs as a result of either direct teaching or observation. In either process, individuals learn to form categories and generalizations and to see relationships among concepts and ideas. For example, when a person who knows that robins and blue jays are birds sees a type he's never seen before, he will still be able to recognize it as a bird. (See also DEVELOPMENTAL PSYCHOLOGY.)

Factors Affecting Learning Complex forms of learning, especially cognitive learning, are affected by several factors. Among these are feedback, transfer, and practice. *Feedback* refers to finding out the results of an action. Receiving feedback increases the ability to learn because it helps an individual avoid repeating mistakes and it provides reinforcement for positive actions. *Transfer* refers to the use of a previously learned skill or behavior to help learn a new one. For example, a person who plays the piano will be able to carry over those skills to learning how to play the organ. In some cases, a previously learned skill may hinder learning by making it more difficult to perform a new task. *Practice* is the repetition of a task. Practice helps connect individual responses, or behaviors, that are part of an action. For instance, practice of a golf swing, from the placement of the hands on the club to the follow-through, will improve a player's smoothness and accuracy. (See also MOTIVATION.)

Learning Disability

A learning disability is any disorder that interferes with a child's ability to learn to read, write, speak, understand language, or do mathematics. It is a fairly common problem that occurs mostly in children who are of average or above-average intelligence. Learning-disabled children can be helped by special classes or additional help in a regular classroom.

Special Education Programs. *Special education programs for children with learning disabilities often focus on a child's strengths in order to help compensate for his or her disability.*

Types of Learning Disabilities One of the most common learning disabilities is *dyslexia,* a reading disorder. Dyslexic children generally have no problem speaking or understanding spoken language but have difficulty with written words. In reading, they may overlook or reverse some letters. Other kinds of learning disorders include dysphasia, difficulty in speaking or understanding spoken language; dysgraphia, difficulty in writing; and dyscalcula, difficulty with mathematics.

Diagnosis and Treatment Parents or teachers may suspect a learning disorder in preschool or elementary children who are slow to develop language or reading skills. A child who shows signs of a learning disability is often evaluated by a team of specialists, which may include a psychologist, neurologist, speech therapist, and an eye or ear specialist. If physical problems are ruled out and a learning disability is diagnosed, the team will recommend an appropriate learning program to help the child manage the disability and do well in school. Some children will be able to overcome their disability, whereas others will have to manage by using devices such as computers, calculators, and tape recorders.

Depending on the type and extent of the disability, the team may recommend that a child be placed in a special education program in which special teaching techniques are used and students receive more individual attention. Or a team may recommend that a child receive supplemental instruction in a regular classroom. Dyslexic children, for example, can benefit from extra help in reading.

Love

Love is a strong emotional attachment one person has for another. People experience different kinds of love, including love for parents and family, love for friends, and romantic love. Love that is mutual and stable provides peace and contentment. If it is one-sided or if it ends, love can be a source of frustration and unhappiness.

People learn to love by being loved, especially by their parents when they are babies. People who have learned that they are worthy of love are often able to form the most satisfying love relationships as they go through life. People also learn to love by observing the loving relationships of others, such as family and friends.

Each type of love is distinct although all share certain characteristics. People who love one another like, respect, and care about one another. They have a strong sense of commitment to one another and a desire for INTIMACY, or sharing. An additional element found in romantic love relationships is physical attraction and passion.

Companionate Love. *The basis of many enduring relationships is companionate love—mutual feelings of affection, admiration, and respect—that has grown stronger over time.*

Romantic Love Psychologists believe that romantic love changes over the course of the relationship. In most cases, at the beginning each partner feels a strong physical attraction and passion for the other and a desire to spend a lot of time with the other. Each tends to be preoccupied with the other. Each partner also experiences a deep longing to be loved in return and an intense fear of rejection.

As time passes, the couple probably will not keep up this intense level of passion. They enter the second kind of love, called *companionate,* or mature, *love.* In this stage, the couple's relationship deepens and is based less on passion and more on companionship, affection, trust, emotional support, good COMMUNICATION, and sharing of interests and responsibilities. Most long-term romantic relationships progress from passionate to mature love.

Infatuation Sometimes romantic love is confused with infatuation. Infatuations do have some of the qualities of romantic love. Feelings are often very intense and passionate and are based on a strong physical attraction. People who are infatuated, however, have unrealistic expectations about the other person, and they are much more concerned about themselves than about the other. In fact, they may not even know the person with whom they are infatuated. Rock stars and sports figures are often the focus of a fan's infatuation. Relationships based on infatuation usually end very quickly.

Mental Health

Mental health refers to a person's ability to cope with events in daily life, function responsibly in society, and experience personal satisfaction and enjoyment. It includes a positive sense of SELF-ESTEEM as well as feelings of contentment and inner peace. Mental health is not a fixed condition, but a continuous process in which an individual is changing, dealing with everyday problems, and moving toward SELF-ACTUALIZATION, an achievement of life goals, and greater self-understanding.

Many Dimensions of Health. *One dimension of mental health is social health, which involves acting responsibly in the roles you play in society.*

Dimensions of Mental Health Mental health has several dimensions, each of which contributes to a person's overall health and well-being. These dimensions include emotional health, intellectual health, social health, and spiritual health. *Emotional health* involves the feelings one has toward oneself and others, as well as toward one's life situation. A person who is emotionally healthy is able to understand his or her emotions and express them appropriately. Such a person can adjust to change, solve problems, and cope successfully. *Intellectual health* involves a person's ability to make effective use of his or her intellectual capacity and to perform as well as possible such functions as evaluating information and making decisions. *Social health* refers to the ability to perform comfortably and effectively within a variety of social roles. It requires an ability to assume RESPONSIBILITY, communicate effectively, and adapt successfully to one's environment. *Spiritual health* involves a person's deepest feelings and VALUES. Spiritual health may be expressed through a deep religious faith, a feeling of oneness with nature, a sense of inner peace, or loving, supportive RELATIONSHIPS. Spiritually healthy individuals act in harmony with their values. They have a purpose in life and are able to experience love, joy, and fulfillment.

HEALTHY CHOICES

Staying Healthy The dimensions of mental health are closely linked, and each one affects the others. Sound emotional health, for example, can enhance social relationships. Maintaining mental health involves balancing these dimensions, developing each one as fully as possible. (See also COMMUNICATION; COPING SKILLS.)

MENTAL ILLNESS

Mental illness refers to any disorder or problem of the mind that damages a person's ability to cope with life. Psychiatrists and psychologists recognize a broad spectrum of mental problems ranging from mild disorders that do not interfere greatly with a person's life to severe disorders that prevent a person from functioning in normal daily activities. Mental illness is a significant public health problem affecting millions of people in the United States.

Classifying Types of Mental Illness The American Psychiatric Association has established a standard classification system for mental disorders. This system, published in a book called *Diagnostic and Statistical Manual of Mental Disorders* (DSM), is used to help health professionals reliably diagnose and treat mental disorders. The book is revised periodically to reflect the latest scientific findings. The most recent edition, DSM-III-R, was published in 1987 (a new edition, DSM-IV, is due in the mid-1990s). The DSM-III-R groups mental illnesses based on similar features (see chart: Major Diagnostic Categories in DSM-III-R).

Another way that psychiatrists and psychologists group mental illnesses is by their severity. *Psychotic disorders* are those in which individuals lose contact with reality, as in SCHIZOPHRENIA. *Nonpsychotic disorders*, which once were grouped under the heading of NEUROSIS, are illnesses (such as ANXIETY DISORDERS) that disturb daily life but usually permit moderate functioning. (See also PSYCHOSIS.)

> Psychotic disorders are illnesses in which individuals lose contact with reality. Nonpsychotic disorders disturb daily life but usually permit moderate functioning.

Mental disorders can also be classified into two broad categories according to cause. The first category consists of symptoms caused by ORGANIC BRAIN DISORDERS, physical conditions that impair the function of the brain. The other category, *functional disorders*, are those mental illnesses (most of the DSM-III-R categories) that are believed to be psychological in origin because no organic cause is apparent.

Treating Mental Illnesses Treatment of mental illnesses may involve some form of PSYCHOTHERAPY, medication (DRUG THERAPY), or a combination of both. Psychotherapy alone or in conjunction with medication can help cure disorders that are not biologically based. The more severe the symptoms, the more likely that medication will be used to help the affected person manage the symptoms. Very seriously ill people, such as those with schizophrenia, may have to be institutionalized to provide the intense level of treatment needed to manage the illness. The length of institutionalized treatment may vary from several days to months to years, depending on the severity of the disorder and the response to therapy.

Also among those who are institutionalized are people declared insane. *Insanity* is a legal term for people who, because of mental illness, have been judged not to be responsible for their actions. (See also ANTISOCIAL PERSONALITY; BIPOLAR DISORDER; DEPRESSION; MULTIPLE PERSONALITY; PARANOIA; PERSONALITY DISORDERS.)

MAJOR DIAGNOSTIC CATEGORIES IN DSM-III-R

Category	Description or common examples
Disorders usually first evident in infancy, childhood, or adolescence	Hyperactivity, eating disorders, tics
Organic mental syndromes and disorders	Problems, such as dementia, caused by physical decline of brain function due to aging, disease, drugs, etc.
Psychoactive substance use disorders	Problems caused by dependence on alcohol or other drugs
Schizophrenia	Severe psychotic disorders marked by major disturbances in perception, language and thought, emotion, and behavior
Delusional (paranoid) disorder	Problems involving persistent delusions (false beliefs), such as of persecution, grandeur, or jealousy
Mood disorders	Bipolar disorder, major depression
Anxiety disorders	Post-traumatic stress disorder, phobias
Somatoform disorders	Hypochondria, conversion disorders
Dissociative disorders	Psychogenic amnesia, multiple personality disorder
Sexual disorders	Sexual dysfunctions such as impotence and sexual deviations such as exhibitionism
Sleep disorders	Insomnia, sleep terrors, hypersomnia
Impulse control disorders not elsewhere classified	Kleptomania, pathological gambling, pyromania
Psychological factors affecting physical condition	Physical problems, such as ulcers or high blood pressure, that are brought on or made worse by psychological factors
Developmental disorders	Mental retardation, autism
Personality disorders	Paranoid personality, antisocial personality, obsessive-compulsive disorder

MENTAL RETARDATION

Mental retardation is below-average general intelligence accompanied by problems functioning in normal everyday situations. Because mental retardation is defined and measured in many ways, its prevalence is difficult to determine.

Mental retardation is most commonly divided into four levels: mild, moderate, severe, and profound (see chart: Levels of Mental Retardation). Physicians determine which level a person falls into by using scores on standardized intelligence (IQ) tests and measures of adaptive behavior—the ability to meet the demands of life.

LEVELS OF MENTAL RETARDATION

Level	Characteristics of mentally retarded people
Mild	They develop more slowly than do most children. However, they are usually fairly independent by the teen years. As adults, they can generally work at undemanding jobs and live independently, but may need assistance occasionally.
Moderate	As children, they are noticeably delayed in their development, especially in speech. As adults, they can learn to take care of themselves but must usually live and work in a sheltered workshop environment.
Severe	They are greatly delayed in all types of childhood development. As adults, they can learn to care for some of their physical needs and perform simple tasks. However, they need considerable supervision in a sheltered environment.
Profound	As children they function minimally in all areas. They may eventually show basic emotional responses and primitive speech and be able to walk. However, they will always need close, constant supervision and care.

Mental retardation may be caused by genetic or biological factors, such as chromosome (structure containing a cell's genetic codes) abnormalities, disorders of body chemistry, or drug or alcohol use by the mother during pregnancy. However, environmental factors present after birth, such as poor diet, poor health, and lack of parental attention, account for as much as 85 percent of the cases of mental retardation. (See also HEREDITY AND ENVIRONMENT; INTELLIGENCE; LEARNING DISABILITY; DOWN SYNDROME, 3; GENETICS, 6.)

MIND

The mind is the human *consciousness*, the function of the brain that makes humans aware of the thoughts, feelings, PERCEPTIONS, images, sensations, and EMOTIONS they have about themselves and the world around them. Experts have long suspected that consciousness is closely linked to higher-level brain activities of the *cerebral cortex,* but the exact nature of that relationship has not yet been discovered.

Waking consciousness allows people to evaluate themselves and their environments, regulate their behaviors and experiences, and make choices about how to act or think.

Consciousness occurs at several levels ranging from fully alert and structured to wandering and unsystematic. At the level of normal waking consciousness, people are actively aware of themselves and of the world around them. Waking consciousness allows people to evaluate themselves and their environments, regulate their behaviors and experiences, and make choices about how to act or think. During waking consciousness, people are able to be selective, blocking out some of the many stimuli that bombard the mind each day in order to concentrate on what is important at the moment.

Other levels of consciousness—generally less structured and less focused—are called *altered*, or alternate, *states of consciousness*. They include activities such as sleep, DREAMS, daydreams, fantasies, hypnotic states, HALLUCINATIONS, BIOFEEDBACK, meditation, and behaviors brought on by the introduction of drugs into the body. Some types of altered states, such as sleep, are naturally occurring. Others such as meditation and biofeedback are methods used to achieve a higher level of awareness and control over the mind and body. In other cases, such as with HYPNOSIS, an individual's effort to achieve an altered state of consciousness may be assisted by another person, usually a professional. The introduction of certain drugs into the body can reduce awareness or may heighten it.

The Unconscious Mind Austrian physician Sigmund Freud was primarily responsible for the idea of the unconscious mind. According to Freud, every personality has a large unconscious component that consists of feelings, thoughts, and experiences that have been repressed and forgotten because they cause emotional pain or conflict. Although these experiences may not be consciously remembered, Freud believed that they have a significant influence on a person's personality and behavior. Although the idea of the unconscious mind is fundamental to the psychoanalytic theories of understanding PERSONALITY, today many psychologists dispute the theory or consider it relatively minor. (See also CENTRAL NERVOUS SYSTEM; SLEEP, 1; DRUG USE AND ABUSE, 7.)

MOTIVATION

Motivation refers to the inner processes that cause people to act the way they do. It involves the underlying factors—needs, desires, interests, and goals—that determine an individual's behavior. The rewards or goals that motivate a person can come from within (such as the good feelings associated with achievement) or from external sources (such as parents offering the keys to the car for getting good grades).

Motivation is difficult for psychologists to study because it is not directly observable. It must be inferred, or determined, from a person's behavior. Supporters of *biological determinism*, one of the oldest theories of motivation, maintain that motivation is based on *instincts* (biologically and genetically predetermined forces). Psychologists following this theory have identified thousands of different instincts, including the instinct for survival, security, love, aggressiveness, and reproduction, that supposedly cause people to act in certain ways. Biological determinism

Motivation. *One psychological theory about why some people perform dangerous activities is that every person is motivated to maintain a preferred level of arousal. For thrill seekers, the best level of stimulation is high.*

has fallen out of favor because it fails to consider the effects of environment on behavior. It also fails to explain why different people behave in so many different ways in similar situations and why the same person may behave differently in the same situation at different times.

Newer theories have observed that motivation is much more complicated than the explanation offered by the biological determinists. These theories vary but generally recognize the role of environment, emotions, and thought in motivating people. Motivation is connected both to the satisfaction of *drives* (internal mechanisms that cause individuals to seek to fulfill certain innate needs) and to the influence of *incentives* (external forces that prompt behavior). People are motivated to satisfy physiological needs such as hunger and thirst, for example. However, people often eat or drink when they are not truly hungry or thirsty; the time of day, for example, or the sight of a dessert tray may prompt a person to eat or drink. People are motivated psychologically and emotionally as well, to satisfy the desire for approval, achievement, or LOVE, on the one hand, or to avoid feeling pain, conflict, loss, failure, shame, or guilt, on the other hand. (See also LEARNING; PROSOCIAL BEHAVIOR; SELF-ACTUALIZATION.)

MULTIPLE PERSONALITY

Multiple personality is a rare disorder in which a person develops two or more distinct personalities. Each personality emerges or dominates at different times, and the transition from one to another is usually sudden, often occurring as a response to emotional stress. Multiple personality disorder is sometimes confused with the psychotic disorder SCHIZOPHRENIA, but the two are unrelated.

The identities in a multiple personality are often not aware of each other. Each has its own name, distinct traits and moods, and

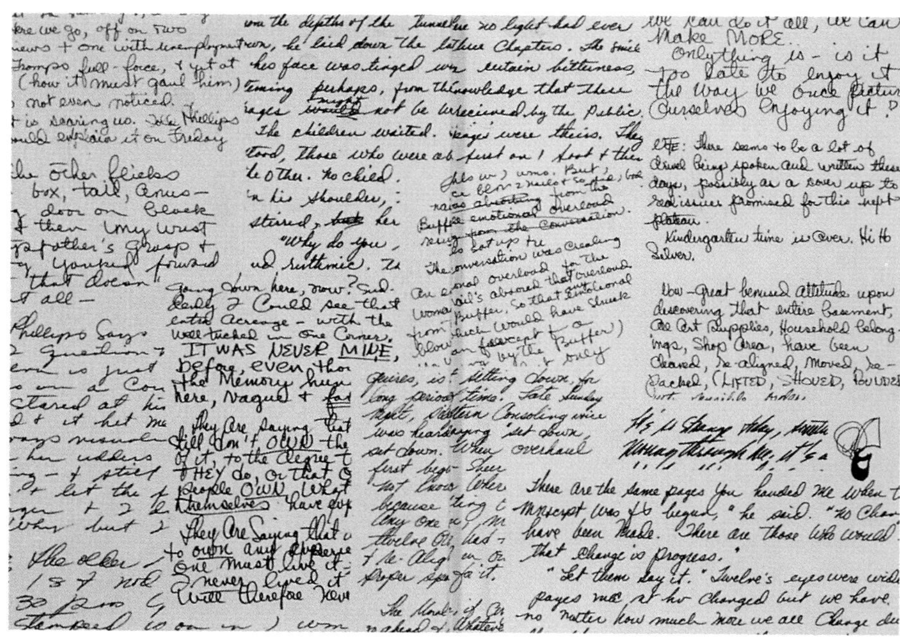

Inside a Multiple Personality. *After beginning psychotherapy in her early forties, Truddi Chase discovered she had more than 90 personalities. She describes the complex interrelationship among her personalities, whom she calls "The Troops," in her book* When Rabbit Howls *by The Troops for Truddi Chase. This unique byline is considered to be the first of its kind in publishing history. Handwriting samples of some of the personalities are shown here.*

independent relationships and memories. The personalities often differ sharply from each other, one being extremely shy and another very outgoing, for example. The personalities may be of different ages, sexes, and races as well. In one documented case, researchers found that the brain wave patterns of the individual personalities were significantly different.

Multiple personality disorder usually begins to develop in early childhood as a result of severe physical, emotional, or sexual abuse. Psychologists believe the separate personalities are a psychological mechanism to escape abuse and the memories of abuse. The disorder is often not recognized or diagnosed until adulthood. People with multiple personalities may become gradually aware of their erratic behavior or of blank periods in their memory.

Two famous cases of multiple personality that became the subjects of books and movies have drawn considerable attention to the disorder. These are *The Three Faces of Eve,* about a woman with 3 personalities, and *Sybil,* about a woman with 16 personalities. Yet there is still debate in the psychiatric community about multiple personalities. Some researchers question whether the disorder really exists. Many others believe that it may be more common than was once believed but often goes unrecognized and undiagnosed.

Treatment Treatment of multiple personality disorder consists of intense PSYCHOTHERAPY to identify the personalities and treat the underlying emotional trauma. The goal of treatment in most cases is to gradually integrate the personalities into one whole personality, although this is a difficult process. The woman on whom *Sybil* was based was treated for 11 years before she was able to integrate her personalities.

NARCISSISM

see PERSONALITY DISORDERS

NEUROSIS

Neurosis is a general term commonly used to refer to a group of relatively mild psychological disorders. A person affected by this type of *nonpsychotic disorder* may be troubled by emotional difficulties but does not lose touch with reality. Neurotic behaviors are often a response to the stress caused by inner conflicts. Currently, psychologists consider the word *neurosis* too broad and too vague a diagnosis to be of assistance in determining the course of treatment for an individual with an emotional problem. (See also ANXIETY; ANXIETY DISORDERS; DEPRESSION; HYPOCHONDRIA; MENTAL ILLNESS; PSYCHOSIS.)

OBSESSIVE/COMPULSIVE

see ANXIETY DISORDERS

Organic Brain Disorders

Organic brain disorders are physical conditions that impair the function of the brain and cause symptoms of mental illness. These disorders, which result in damaged or destroyed brain tissue or an imbalance of chemicals in the brain, can affect a person's emotions, behavior, and thought processes, including memory, reasoning, and judgment.

Causes of Organic Brain Disorders Many physical disorders cause organic brain disorders. Stroke, brain tumor, head injury, and brain hemorrhage may cause memory loss, general confusion, difficulty in concentrating, mood swings, and inappropriate emotional reactions. Alzheimer's disease, a degenerative brain disorder, causes short-term or immediate memory loss, severe mental confusion, and mood and personality changes. It may also cause HALLUCINATIONS and delusions. When infections such as encephalitis and syphilis affect the brain, they may also cause symptoms of a mental disorder, such as personality and behavior changes, confusion, and memory loss. AIDS-related dementia results from infection of brain tissue by HIV.

RISK FACTORS ▶ ▶ ▶ ▶ ▶ ▶

Heavy use of alcohol, drugs, or other chemicals can cause many symptoms of mental illness. *Delirium tremens,* which usually occurs as a result of withdrawal from alcohol after heavy use, is marked by distortion of PERCEPTIONS, delusion, hallucination, confusion, and a high level of anxiety. Drugs such as cocaine, LSD, and amphetamines can cause symptoms of schizophrenia, including delusions, hallucinations, and confusion.

Treatment Because organic brain disorders have the same symptoms as psychologically based illnesses, a person with symptoms of mental illness should be checked to see whether his or her symptoms are due to physical causes. Treatment will depend on the specific organic illness. Sometimes the symptoms of mental illness, such as delirium caused by infection, will disappear when the organic disorder is treated. In other cases, as with an incurable disease like Alzheimer's, the symptoms worsen as the disease progresses. Treatment in these cases is supportive, helping the affected person and family adjust to the illness. (See also SENILITY; ALZHEIMER'S DISEASE, 3; BRAIN TUMOR, 3; DEMENTIA, 3; STROKE, 3; DELIRIUM TREMENS, 7.)

Panic Attack

see ANXIETY DISORDERS

Paranoia

Paranoia is a mental disorder characterized by secretiveness, suspiciousness, jealousy, and persistent delusions (false beliefs) of persecution or grandeur. A person who develops this paranoid disorder imagines that the behaviors of others are menacing. He or she is overly sensitive to criticism, denying personal responsibility for any problems and shifting blame to others. Emotional warmth and openness and a sense of humor are often lacking as well. A person who exhibits mild paranoia may lead a

Paranoid Disorder. *A person who develops paranoid disorder may believe that other people are dangerous.*

relatively normal life. With severe paranoia, however, judgment and perception often deteriorate to the point that all aspects of behavior are adversely affected. Treatment of paranoia is difficult because paranoid people do not think that they have a problem. In some cases, the use of antipsychotic drugs is helpful.

Paranoid thinking is a symptom of several other mental disorders, particularly *paranoid personality disorder* and paranoid SCHIZOPHRENIA. It may also be one of the symptoms of *schizotypal personality disorder.* Symptoms of paranoia are also an element in some ORGANIC BRAIN DISORDERS. Paranoid symptoms may be brought on by drug intoxication. As with all mental disorders, organic causes of paranoid behavior must be ruled out before attributing them to a psychological cause. (See also DRUG THERAPY; PERSONALITY DISORDERS.)

PEER PRESSURE

Peer pressure is the influence exerted by your own age or social group (your *peers*) to conform, or be like others in the group. Identification with peers is normal behavior in early adolescence, when teenagers adopt styles and behaviors that set them apart from other age groups—especially their parents. Studies show that CONFORMITY with peers peaks at ages 12 to 13.

For adolescents, identification with peers has the greatest effect in such areas as dress, taste in music, speech, and mannerisms. Teens crave acceptance from their peers and often want to project a particular image. As a result, peer pressure can also encourage behaviors such as smoking cigarettes, drinking alcohol, using drugs, becoming sexually active, and other actions that may be unhealthy and potentially dangerous, but which teens may view as approved of by their peers.

Feeling a part of a peer group is an important aspect of adolescent development. By identifying with a group of peers, young people can support one another as they define themselves and move toward independence

Peer Influence. *Influence from people your own age can have positive aspects as well as negative ones.*

from their parents. In addition, interacting with a peer group helps young people gain social experience while differentiating themselves from adults.

Parents may view a teenager's apparent conformity to a peer group as a sign that the teen is rejecting parental VALUES. Studies show, however, that parental influence remains important, especially concerning issues like basic values and future goals. The influence of parents continues to be strong into adulthood.

PERCEPTION

Perception is the process by which the brain interprets sensory information from the environment. Without your being aware of it, your brain organizes stimuli from the senses of sight, sound, smell, taste, and touch and gives them meaning. In order for perception to take place, you must receive information from the external world through your body's sensory *receptors* (the eyes, ears, nose, mouth, and skin). The information travels along the neural pathways of the nervous system to your brain, which interprets, or perceives, it. Together, your senses and perception enable you to interact with and adapt to your environment. They are the basis for all psychological processes, such as LEARNING, problem solving, and COMMUNICATION. Distorted perceptions can be a sign of mental illness.

Influence of Expectation on Perception. *If people are told that this is a picture of a rabbit, they will probably agree. If, however, they are told that they are looking at a picture of a bird, they will probably perceive a bird.*

Each person receives sensations and perceives them in different ways. One factor affecting the development of perceptual processes is the level at which the senses are functioning. For example, people who have inherited color blindness do not sense and perceive all colors the same as individuals with normal color vision do. Perceptions are also affected by the knowledge a person has gained through learning and experience and by a person's expectations (see illustration: Influence of Expectation on Perception). For example, a person who lives in an abusive environment and has learned to be watchful for signs of potential abuse may tend to interpret others' behavior as more threatening than someone from a more nurturing environment would. In this case, experience and expectations cause one person's perceptions to differ from another's.

PERSONALITY

Personality can be defined as the distinctive patterns of thoughts, behaviors, and emotions that characterize a person's responses to the events and situations encountered in life. Psychologists who study personality have developed a number of theories to explain the differences between individuals. These personality theories attempt to identify behavior patterns and to explain why people react differently in similar situations.

Trait Theories According to the advocates of trait theories, each individual has a set of relatively stable personality traits, or characteristics, that influence actions and behavior. These traits prompt consistent responses in different situations. For example, a person who is competitive in one situation is likely to be competitive in another situation as well. People differ according to the degree to which they possess a particular trait. Some psychologists believe that an individual's personality can be explained in terms of a few basic core traits that affect all other personality characteristics. A core trait of high self-confidence, for example, may be the basis for characteristics such as ASSERTIVENESS and independence. Other psychologists believe that personality can be reduced to even fewer traits. One trait theory explains personality differences in terms of two basic dimensions: stability/instability, the degree to which people have control over their feelings, and extroversion/introversion, the extent to which people are socially outgoing or withdrawn.

Psychoanalytic Theories Psychoanalytic theories, which began with the work of Sigmund Freud, emphasize the importance of childhood experiences in shaping personality. They contend that early experiences buried in the *unconscious mind* form the basis of motives and feelings of which the individual is unaware. Personality differences among individuals are the result of the unconscious motives that drive a person's conscious actions and behavior.

Behavioral Theories Behavioral theories explain personality differences as the result of learning through rewards and punishments. According to these theories, individuals differ in their learning experiences and for that reason develop different behaviors and different personalities. Behavioral theorists would not try to explain an individual's antisocial personality by analyzing feelings resulting from unconscious childhood experiences. Instead, they look for explanations in observable

Personality Differences. *Through personality theories, psychologists attempt to explain why people react differently in similar situations.*

events or situations, such as the child-rearing practices of parents. Behavioral theorists are less concerned with understanding the structure of personality than with predicting and controlling behavior.

Humanistic Theories Humanistic theories of personality emphasize the uniqueness of each individual and the importance of SELF-IMAGE. Humanistic theorists see people as basically good and believe they possess a drive for SELF-ACTUALIZATION—the realization of their potential as individuals. The humanists believe that many people begin learning at an early age to distort or suppress certain feelings or behaviors in order to be accepted by others. Consequently, these people come to feel that love or acceptance from others is conditional, which tends to lower their self-confidence and SELF-ESTEEM. A person's true inner nature can become distorted because of low self-esteem or a perceived gap between a person's self-image and what he or she aspires to be.

Personality and Health Personality may play a significant role in overall health and well-being. Some psychologists believe that behaviors associated with certain personality types, called Type A and Type B, can affect health. The *Type A* personality is characterized by impatience, competitiveness, hostility, and aggressiveness. People with *Type B* personalities, on the other hand, are more low-key and relaxed. Studies have linked Type A personalities with high levels of STRESS and increased rates of heart disease. (See also ADULT IDENTITY; ATTITUDES; PERSONALITY DISORDERS; PSYCHOLOGY.)

PERSONALITY DISORDERS

Personality disorders are character traits or patterns of behavior that interfere with a person's ability to relate to others or cope effectively with his or her environment. These traits and patterns of behavior are long lasting and consistent. They prevent the person from functioning adequately in social or work situations or cause the person intense distress. Treatment may be difficult because some people with personality disorders are not bothered by their behavioral patterns and have little desire to change. Personality disorders usually first become apparent during adolescence or earlier and usually continue throughout adulthood.

Types of Personality Disorders *Paranoid personality disorder* is characterized by a sense of PARANOIA, a suspiciousness and mistrust of other people. A person with this disorder expects to be harmed by others and becomes secretive as a result. Paranoid personalities are extremely jealous, overly sensitive, and argumentative. They are ready to blame others even for things that are their fault.

A person with *schizoid personality disorder* is withdrawn and may appear dull and without emotional warmth. Such individuals often do not react either to praise or to criticism, and they appear unconcerned about the feelings of others. They often pursue solitary interests and may daydream a great deal. *Schizotypal personality disorder* is characterized by a lack of personal relationships, and by eccentricity in thinking, sensory perception, speech, and behavior.

Narcissistic Personality Disorder. *The word* narcissistic *comes from the Greek mythological character Narcissus, who fell in love with his own reflection.*

Individuals with *histrionic personality disorder* are overly dramatic, expressing emotions in exaggerated ways that call attention to themselves. Although charming on the surface, they have trouble forming meaningful relationships because they are inconsiderate, manipulative, and demanding.

Narcissistic personality disorder is characterized by an exaggerated sense of self-importance. People with this disorder are extremely self-centered and preoccupied with fantasies of success. They need the attention and admiration of others, but they take advantage of others and feel entitled to accept favors without reciprocating.

People with certain personality disorders display a particular FEAR or ANXIETY. For example, individuals with *avoidant personality disorder* are overly sensitive to the possibility of rejection or humiliation. They suffer from low self-esteem and are quick to deny or criticize their own achievements. People with *dependent personality disorder* lack self-confidence and self-reliance. They rely on others to make important decisions for them and put the needs of others above their own. They are submissive and unable to make demands of others. *Compulsive personality disorder* is characterized by a preoccupation with rules, order, and efficiency. People with this disorder are perfectionists and demand that things be done their way. They lack personal warmth and the ability to enjoy informal social and recreational activities. People with *passive-aggressive personality disorder* resist, indirectly, the demands of others. They procrastinate (put things off), are usually late, and "forget" to respond to others. Their resistance is actually an aggressive and hostile way of controlling others.

One of the most troubling disorders is ANTISOCIAL PERSONALITY disorder. This disorder includes persistent patterns of impulsive, selfish, and immoral behavior and often results in criminal activity. (See also MENTAL ILLNESS; PSYCHOTHERAPY; SCHIZOPHRENIA.)

PHOBIA

see ANXIETY DISORDERS

POST-TRAUMATIC STRESS DISORDER

Post-traumatic stress disorder (PTSD) is a type of ANXIETY DISORDER that follows an extremely disturbing event, one outside the realm of normal human experience. The event (the *trauma*) may be some form of violence, a natural disaster, or warfare. The time needed to overcome the ANXIETY depends on several factors, including the individual's personality, the amount of emotional support available from friends and family, and the original trauma. The disorder may clear up within weeks, but in severe cases it may last for years.

Military combat is a common cause of PTSD. Once called combat fatigue or shell shock, the disorder affects members of the armed forces who have suffered through the ordeals of combat. Survivors of plane

Post-Traumatic Stress Disorder. *Rescue workers are sometimes called on to give aid in gruesome catastrophic situations. As a result of their experiences, some develop post-traumatic stress disorder.*

crashes, mass shooting sprees, and rape have also been affected, as have rescue workers whose jobs place them in the midst of great suffering or tragedy (see illustration: Post-Traumatic Stress Disorder).

The symptoms of PTSD include FEAR, nightmares, flashbacks, nervousness, insomnia, difficulty concentrating, and DEPRESSION. People with PTSD often become emotionally numb, feeling detached from others and unable to gain pleasure from things they once enjoyed. The anxiety may begin right after the event, or it may take months to set in.

Numerous sources of treatment are now available for people with PTSD. Training sessions for workers and counseling sessions for survivors help individuals who have experienced tragic events, natural disasters, and violent crimes cope with the trauma. Psychologists emphasize that symptoms of anxiety are a normal response to traumatic events. Counseling and emotional support can help people overcome these symptoms. Prevention of PTSD by immediate crisis counseling is especially important. (See also CRISIS INTERVENTION; STRESS.)

PREJUDICE

Prejudice is a negative and hurtful ATTITUDE people have toward individuals simply because they are members of a particular group. Prejudice, which literally means "a decision made in advance," is based on false or incomplete information. A whole group is judged to be the same despite individual differences. Ethnic and racial minorities are common targets of prejudice as are women, old people, and those who are overweight or disabled. Prejudicial beliefs and ideas are very harmful and difficult to change.

Some people form their attitudes about groups of people on the basis of *stereotypes*. These are preconceived, exaggerated, or untrue images or beliefs that people hold about all of the members of a group, such as believing that all women are poor decision makers. Stereotypes are a simplistic and convenient way for people to sort and classify information. However, such beliefs are harmful because they keep people from seeing and appreciating individual differences. When people believe in a stereotype, they usually reject any new information that does not conform to the stereotype, or they tend to believe that the new information is merely an "exception to the rule."

Causes of Prejudice There are a number of theories about why people form prejudices. According to the *scapegoat theory,* people who are unhappy with their lives take out their frustration and anger against a less powerful minority group (the scapegoat). During the 1930s in Germany, for example, bad economic times led German leaders to blame Jews for the country's hard times. A similar theory, the *competition theory,* says that prejudice stems from the competition between groups of people for jobs and other resources. The groups develop an "us against them" attitude. Historically, prejudice against minority groups increases during hard times. Still another theory claims that when there is inequality of status within a society, prejudices arise to justify keeping certain groups "down."

People learn prejudicial attitudes from friends and family; from teachers; and from images in movies, on television, and in books and periodicals. These learned attitudes may be handed down from generation to generation just as other kinds of beliefs and information are.

Kinds of Prejudice *Racism,* prejudice directed against a specific race or ethnic group, is one of the most common kinds of prejudice. Nearly every racial and ethnic group that has immigrated to the United States has experienced racism at one time or another. Racism is still widespread against African-Americans, Hispanics, and more recent immigrant groups such as Southeast Asians, Arabs, and Pakistanis. *Sexism* is also very common in the United States. Sexism is prejudice against a person based on the person's sex. It is usually used to describe prejudice against women. *Ageism* refers to prejudice against the elderly. It is characterized by the view that older people are incompetent, useless, or senile.

Results of Prejudice. *Prejudicial attitudes by individuals toward other groups can result in violent confrontations.*

The Results of Prejudice Prejudice leads to *discrimination,* or harmful action based on prejudicial beliefs. Both individuals and governments practice discrimination. Discrimination has kept people out of jobs and schools, segregated them in certain neighborhoods, and denied them basic civil rights. As a result, individuals who are discriminated against may have low SELF-ESTEEM and may experience financial and health problems. They must often cope with feelings of fear, anger, depression, and despair.

Reducing Prejudice Prejudicial attitudes are difficult, but not impossible, to change. When people from different groups get to know one another as individuals and live or work on an equal basis, prejudice and stereotypes usually lessen. Interdependence and cooperation among groups is important. Studies have found that negative attitudes tend to disappear when people of different groups must depend on one another for survival or success. In daily life, parents and educators can promote attitudes such as tolerance and respect for others to reduce prejudice. Individuals can challenge the appropriateness of prejudicial remarks or actions from acquaintances, friends, or family members.

Prosocial Behavior

Prosocial behavior, also known as *altruism,* involves performing some act that helps others but provides no obvious benefit for the person who is helping. Prosocial behavior includes a broad range of activities such as donating blood, giving to charities, or saving someone from danger.

What prompts people to act prosocially is the subject of much speculation and research. Experts have found little evidence that humans have an innate tendency to help one another. Rather, they believe that prosocial behavior is largely a result of learning and is heavily influenced by circumstances and conscious decisions. For example, for a person to act to save someone from danger, that person must first notice that something is happening and realize that help is needed in the situation. The person must then decide to accept responsibility for helping.

In some situations, a phenomenon known as *diffusion of responsibility* may prevent people from helping. Studies show that when a single person witnesses a situation in which help is required, that person feels a great responsibility. When a number of people are present, however, the responsibility becomes diffused, or spread out, among the group, and each individual assumes that someone else will provide the necessary assistance.

Other factors that may affect prosocial behavior are mood and STRESS. When people are in good moods and have low levels of stress, they are more likely to help others.

Working for Others. *People who volunteer their time to help others are exhibiting prosocial behavior. Experts believe that such behavior is learned rather than innate.*

Psychiatry

Psychiatry is the area of medicine that studies, diagnoses, treats, and prevents mental illness and behavioral and emotional problems. This medical specialty is practiced by *psychiatrists*, medical doctors who have completed a residency in psychiatry. By virtue of a medical degree, psychiatrists differ from psychologists, nonmedical practitioners who also study and treat behavioral and emotional problems.

Psychiatrists. *Psychiatrists are qualified to treat mental disorders that have both physiological and psychological causes.*

Because of their medical training, psychiatrists can use biologically based methods of therapy such as DRUG THERAPY and ELECTROCONVULSIVE THERAPY to treat patients. They can also use PSYCHOTHERAPY, or psychologically based therapy. Thus, psychiatrists are able to treat mental disorders that have both physiological and psychological causes. Many psychiatrists who practice therapy use *psychoanalysis*, a method developed by Sigmund Freud to help patients uncover and resolve problems and conflicts buried in their unconscious MIND. Other psychiatrists use *humanistic therapies*, *cognitive therapy*, and *behavior therapy*. (See PSYCHOTHERAPY for discussion of these methods.)

The field of psychiatry includes a number of specialties. Neuropsychiatry, for example, is a specialty that treats both the psychological and physiological disorders that affect the nervous system. Child psychiatry and geriatric psychiatry each focus on a particular group of people. Some areas of psychiatry focus on the social aspects of mental health. These include *social psychiatry*, which examines the connection between mental illness and the social environment, and *community psychiatry*, which involves developing and coordinating mental health services in the community. (See also PSYCHOLOGY; PSYCHOTHERAPISTS, 9.)

Psychology

Psychology is the study of behavior and mental processes. Psychologists are trained to observe and analyze behavior and to apply their knowledge to influence behavior. Although best known in their role as counselors helping people solve mental and emotional problems, psychologists also teach and conduct research. They work in private industry and business, in colleges and universities, in health-care facilities, and in government agencies.

Psychology and PSYCHIATRY are closely related and specialists from the two fields often work together, but the training for the two fields is different. *Psychologists* typically have earned a Ph.D. or Psy.D. (doctor of psychology) during 4 to 6 years of postgraduate training, whereas *psychiatrists* are medical doctors (M.D.'s) with advanced training in psychiatric medicine. Psychiatrists can prescribe medication for their patients; psychologists cannot. Psychologists receive extensive training in psychological testing and assessment, whereas psychiatrists have more training in the area of neurological diagnosis.

A Brief History Although people have speculated about mental processes and behavior for centuries, the beginnings of modern psychology are traced to the late 1800s. Wilhelm Wundt in Germany and William James in the United States were the first to establish psychology as a separate field of study. At about the same time, Sigmund Freud in Austria developed a way of treating mental illness that is still used today. Freud's method, known as *psychoanalysis,* is an attempt to treat troubling mental and physical symptoms by resolving conflicts in the unconscious mind. Another way of dealing with mental illness is found in behaviorism. *Behaviorism* focuses on observable behavior and tries to explain how

Social Psychology. *People are influenced by those around them. The behavior of people in groups is one area of interest to psychologists in the field of social psychology.*

that behavior is controlled by stimuli in the environment. The Russian physiologist Ivan Pavlov and Americans John B. Watson and B. F. Skinner were important theorists in behavioral psychology. *Humanistic psychology* takes an entirely different approach, emphasizing the importance of the fulfillment of individual potential. Abraham Maslow and Carl Rogers are leading figures in humanistic psychology.

Fields of Specialization Today, psychology includes many specialties and subspecialties, a few of which are discussed here. Two of the largest fields of psychology are *clinical psychology* and *counseling psychology.* Psychologists in these two fields study, diagnose and treat a wide range of problems affecting mental health. Clinical psychologists may deal with problems from mild anxiety to serious psychological disorders. Counseling psychologists often work to help people function well in daily life, perhaps through career, rehabilitation, marriage, or aging counseling. Many psychologists in these fields work in private practice or in hospitals and clinics treating individuals in one-to-one therapy and counseling sessions.

Today, psychology includes many specialties and subspecialties. Two of the largest fields of psychology are clinical psychology and counseling psychology.

Psychologists involved in *experimental psychology* design experiments and conduct research, usually in laboratory settings. They study behavior, motivation, learning, and thinking. Experimental psychologists conduct studies under controlled conditions to explain and predict behavior. The term *experimental psychology* is somewhat misleading, because psychologists in other fields also use experimental methods extensively.

Social psychology studies how the behavior of individuals is influenced by those around them. Social psychologists are concerned with how people behave in groups (for example, how leaders emerge), how people see others, and why people conform.

School psychologists are employed in elementary and secondary school districts. Their work includes training teachers to handle problems with students, counseling students and sometimes their families, and giving standardized achievement and psychological tests and evaluating the results. They also intervene when there is a disaster or crisis, such as a bus accident, that affects the school.

DEVELOPMENTAL PSYCHOLOGY looks at how behavior changes as a person grows from infancy through adulthood. Some developmental psychologists study particular age-groups, such as early childhood or adolescence.

The field of *industrial and organizational psychology* is concerned with people in the workplace. It studies psychological factors in industry, such as employee selection and training, worker satisfaction, and effective leadership. These psychologists work toward improving morale and working conditions, preventing accidents on the job, and creating tests that match people with suitable jobs.

The specialty of *neuropsychology* studies the connection between the brain and human behavior. In a related field, *psychopharmacologists* study the effects of drugs on behavior as they impact on the brain and the rest of the nervous system.

The relationship between the environment and behavior is the focus of *environmental psychology.* Psychologists in this field study the way air pollution, loud noise, or urban crowding affect behavior. They may be asked to provide expert advice to people who design buildings or plan cities. (See also CONDITIONING; PSYCHOTHERAPY; PSYCHOTHERAPISTS, **9**.)

PSYCHOPATH

see ANTISOCIAL PERSONALITY

PSYCHOPHARMACOLOGY

see DRUG THERAPY

PSYCHOSIS

Psychosis refers to a serious mental disorder in which individuals lose contact with reality. A psychotic disorder is generally characterized by severely distorted ideas and perceptions. In many cases, these ideas take the form of *delusions* (false beliefs that are maintained despite strong evidence to the contrary) and HALLUCINATIONS (hearing or seeing things that are not there). In addition, speech may be irrational, and emotions may swing inappropriately between extremes. Individuals with a psychotic disorder often cannot perform normal daily tasks and may have to be hospitalized because they are a danger to themselves or others. SCHIZOPHRENIA is a psychosis as are some forms of major DEPRESSION. Besides psychological factors, possible causes of psychosis include hereditary factors, a chemical imbalance, and withdrawal from an addictive drug. Treatment usually involves the use of DRUG THERAPY. (See also MENTAL ILLNESS; NEUROSIS.)

PSYCHOSOMATIC DISORDERS

A psychosomatic disorder is any illness that is caused or made worse by psychological factors. Psychosomatic disorders are directly related to STRESS. Emotional problems, worries, or unpleasant events can produce real physical symptoms or diseases.

Many disorders may have a psychosomatic component. Among those in which stress may play a significant role are headaches, backaches, nausea, cold sores, skin conditions such as eczema, peptic ulcers, asthma, and hypertension. In many other diseases, psychosomatic factors may act indirectly by affecting the immune system and lowering the body's resistance to disease. Thus stress may play a role in diabetes, heart disease, cancer, and autoimmune disorders such as rheumatoid arthritis.

Psychosomatic disorders are real illnesses, but the term is often confused with *somatoform disorders*, a group of psychological disorders marked by imaginary symptoms. The two main types of somatoform disorders are conversion disorder and hypochondria (or hypochondriasis). A person with *conversion disorder* converts repressed emotions or ANXIETY into a loss of physical function, such as paralysis or blindness. A person with HYPOCHONDRIA is basically in good health but is preoccupied with imaginary ailments.

Treatment Treating psychosomatic disorders requires treating the physical disorder first. PSYCHOTHERAPY may also be prescribed in order to hasten recovery and avoid further attacks of the illness. (See also HYSTERIA.)

PSYCHOTHERAPY

Psychotherapy is the treatment of psychological disorders through the use of psychological principles and techniques. Trained therapists, which include psychiatrists, psychologists, and other psychotherapists, work with clients to help them understand their problems, themselves, and their environment. Therapists offer hope, compassion, and understanding as they guide their clients toward solutions to problems affecting emotions, behavior, or thought. Some therapists work to help clients replace feelings of ANXIETY, DEPRESSION, and low self-esteem with feelings of security, hope, and self-confidence. Others work to help clients change behavior through developing insight or new behavioral patterns.

When a mental disorder is caused by physiological conditions, *biological therapies* may be used. Because biological therapies involve the use of drugs, electroconvulsive shock, and psychosurgery, they may be done only by medical doctors.

Psychologically based psychotherapy includes psychoanalysis and cognitive, behavioral, and humanistic therapies. Psychotherapists most often meet with their clients alone. Occasionally, groups of clients who have similar problems meet with one or more therapists. Some therapists specialize in counseling married couples and families.

> There are four major types of psychologically based psychotherapy: psychoanalytic, cognitive, behavioral, and humanistic.

Psychologically Based Psychotherapies There are four major types of psychologically based psychotherapy: psychoanalytic, cognitive, behavioral, and humanistic. Each is briefly described below. The focus and emphasis of the techniques used by a therapist to help a client vary according to the psychological theory practiced by the therapist.

Psychoanalysis was developed by Sigmund Freud early in the twentieth century. Freud believed that mental disorders resulted from lack of normal emotional development in childhood. His treatment helped patients relive experiences from early childhood in order to uncover and resolve any problems and conflicts that were buried in the unconscious MIND. Techniques used by Freud and his successors involve *free association* (random expression of seemingly unrelated thoughts) and interpretation of the patient's DREAMS. These techniques are used to bring out repressed emotions and resolve unconscious conflicts. Today, few psychoanalysts follow Freud's techniques strictly. Many practice a modified type of psychoanalysis, called psychodynamic therapy, that lasts for a shorter period of time and is less intensive. Modern psychodynamic therapies still look for deep, unconscious conflicts rooted in childhood experiences, but they also consider the impact on behavior of current social influences and interpersonal relationships.

Cognitive therapy is based on the view that emotional problems stem from an individual's mistaken beliefs and distorted thoughts about himself or herself and about the world. The therapist's role is to find out what the client's irrational or counterproductive thoughts are and help the client think more positively and productively. Cognitive therapy is also referred to as cognitive behavior therapy because it assumes that once clients change the way they think, they will be able to behave more rationally.

Behavior therapy focuses on changing disturbing ways of acting so that people can function better. Behavior therapists believe that people learn how to behave inappropriately and ineffectively. Therefore, they can be taught to adopt new, productive behaviors. Behavior therapists use LEARNING techniques that employ, among other methods, several types of CONDITIONING. Conditioning alters behavior by teaching people to change their response to a fearful or annoying stimulus (a particular person, object, or event) or by changing the consequences of a behavior. Behavioral therapy is often used to treat *phobias* (excessive fear of an object or situation), drug or alcohol abuse, and eating disorders.

Humanistic therapies help people realize their potential by giving them the tools needed to work toward SELF-ACTUALIZATION and growth. Humanistic therapists believe there is minimal influence from childhood conflicts and from external events on a person's behavior. They believe that individuals are ultimately free to make the choices that affect their behavior. *Person-centered therapy,* a humanistic therapy developed by American psychologist Carl Rogers, leads clients to self-understanding by helping them learn to value who they really are. *Gestalt therapy,* developed by German psychoanalyst Fritz Perls, is another example of a humanistic therapy that works toward self-awareness. It considers past

Group Therapy. *Group therapy offers people a valuable type of treatment that is usually less expensive than individual treatment because the therapist devotes time to several patients at once, resulting in a lower fee per person.*

conflicts to be important only if they have an effect on an individual's present behavior. Gestalt therapists encourage clients to take responsibility for their own feelings and actions rather than blaming behavior on traumas that occurred in the past.

> In group therapy, a therapist can help foster better interpersonal relationships by encouraging people to interact and share their experiences.

Group Therapy Usually, therapists meet with clients in one-to-one sessions. In some cases, however, one or more therapists use the technique of treating people in groups. When a therapist treats a group of people who share similar problems, he or she can help foster better interpersonal relationships by encouraging people to interact and share their experiences. Each individual benefits from emotional support provided by the group and can learn from the behavior of group members who are starting to cope with problems successfully. Group therapy seems particularly effective in treating drug addiction, alcoholism, and obesity.

Marriage therapy and *family therapy* are special types of group therapy that treat a couple or an entire family together. Often couples enter marriage therapy when they are thinking about divorce. In many cases, families enter therapy as part of a treatment program for one member whose problems (such as mental illness or addiction to drugs or gambling) are disturbing the functioning of the family. Therapy may stress the interactions of family members and examine how members' faulty reactions and defensive patterns influence each person's behavior and family roles. Marriage and family therapy may involve trying to improve relationships and skills for solving problems and settling conflicts by encouraging family members to communicate in more open and honest ways.

Biologically Based Psychotherapies Biologically based therapies assume that problem behaviors are caused, at least in part, by chemical imbalances or by a disturbance in the functioning of the nervous system. Because biological therapies involve prescribing drugs and performing medical procedures, they can be performed only by medical doctors, particularly psychiatrists and neurologists.

DRUG THERAPY, the use of chemicals to treat psychological disorders, is employed in the treatment of a range of abnormal behaviors either by correcting chemical imbalances in the nervous system or by relieving symptoms of psychological problems. Types of drug therapy include *antianxiety drugs* to treat anxiety disorders; *antipsychotic drugs* to reduce delusions and hallucinations that are symptoms of schizophrenia and other disorders; and *antidepressant drugs* to relieve depression. Since the development of drug therapy in the 1950s, the incidence of electroconvulsive therapy and psychosurgery have dropped dramatically. Its development was also responsible for a dramatic reduction in the number of people committed to mental institutions.

ELECTROCONVULSIVE THERAPY (ECT) (also called shock therapy) involves placing electrodes on one or both sides of the head and passing an electrical current into the brain. The current triggers a firing of neurons in the brain and causes a convulsion. Used in the 1940s and 1950s to treat numerous types of psychological disorders, ECT is a procedure that is used mainly to relieve depression in patients who have not responded to medication.

Psychosurgery includes operations performed on the brain to relieve severe mental symptoms that have not been helped by other types of treatment. A technique called a *lobotomy* involves cutting the nerve fibers between areas of the frontal lobes of the brain. Because this procedure radically alters the brain and affects personality, it is now rarely used. (See also PSYCHIATRY; PSYCHOLOGY.)

RELATIONSHIPS

Relationships include all the connections individuals establish with other people. They encompass a variety of attachments, including superficial relationships formed with coworkers, close relationships with FAMILY and friends, and romantic relationships.

Relationships allow people to share recreation and sports, common interests, and personal celebrations. Friends, family, and lovers provide emotional support to help individuals through difficult experiences, thus contributing to happiness and health. Close relationships help fulfill basic needs for belonging and LOVE. Any relationship—whether with friends, relatives, or lovers—involves hard work, commitment, compromise, and a willingness to stay together during difficult as well as good times.

The Impact of Relationships Close relationships can be a source of support and strength from childhood through adulthood. Relationships within a family form an individual's first important social network. Early

Moving Away. *The highly mobile nature of today's society often makes it difficult to maintain strong relationships.*

nurturing and parent-child interactions provide a pattern of relating that tends to endure throughout life. Relationships with siblings are often complex. They frequently involve both negative and positive feelings. Rivalry and conflict can combine with feelings of love and loyalty. This complexity, however, offers siblings opportunities to learn how to deal with anger and aggression while maintaining a relationship. (See also SIBLING RIVALRY.)

Although family relationships remain strong, the peer group becomes increasingly important in older childhood and adolescence. FRIENDSHIPS with peers are particularly important to adolescent development, providing support as teenagers move toward adulthood and independence from their parents.

Love relationships provide opportunities for the development of INTIMACY: the sharing of experiences, personal feelings, and sexual closeness. An intimate relationship, in which each person gives and receives understanding and a sense of being valued, is a goal that most people pursue.

During the development stage of a relationship, people spend increasing amounts of time with each other, making a commitment to the other person.

The Stages of a Relationship Relationships involving close friends and lovers typically follow three distinct stages: development, maintenance, and dissolution. During the *development* stage, people spend increasing amounts of time with each other, making a commitment to the other person. During this stage, people in relationships tend to share feelings and develop trust.

During the *maintenance* stage, people find ways to resolve the conflicts that inevitably arise. Research shows that the ability to resolve conflict is more important for developing intimacy than the ability simply to avoid conflict or remove it from the relationship. Another aspect of successful maintenance is being available to help the other person when he or she needs emotional support.

Some relationships reach the *dissolution,* or ending, stage. When relationships end, they do so for many reasons. Romantic relationships may end when one of the partners becomes interested in someone else. Friendships can be strained by new friends and new interests. In addition, the highly mobile nature of some segments of today's society, in which people move frequently, makes it difficult to maintain strong relationships.

Harmful Relationships Sometimes people become involved in relationships that are harmful to themselves or to the other person in the relationship. These include relationships in which there is emotional, physical, or sexual abuse. Such relationships must be dissolved or completely altered in order for either partner to recover.

In recent years there has been much discussion of codependent relationships. *Codependency* was originally identified as a type of relationship typical of spouses of alcoholics. The term has now been widened to refer to any relationship in which one person is so preoccupied with meeting the needs of the other person that his or her own needs are not met. The term has also been used to describe people who have relationships with a mentally disturbed or chronically ill person or with a rebellious or troubled child. The codependent partner acts as the "rescuer" of the other partner, supporting that person's unhealthy behavior. Help for people involved in codependent relationships focuses on having the codependent partner heighten his or her own self-esteem and learn to set limits on the relationship. (See also CONFLICT RESOLUTION; SOCIAL SKILLS; CODEPENDENCY, 7.)

Relaxation Training

Relaxation training is a means of coping with stress and stress-related illnesses. It involves learning one of several techniques to relax the muscles and mind. The most common techniques are progressive relaxation, relaxation response, autogenic training, meditation, and BIOFEEDBACK. Relaxation training can be useful in relieving high blood pressure, headaches, sleep disorders, migraine headaches, and muscle tension.

Traditional Methods. *Meditation and yoga are both traditional relaxation methods.*

Progressive relaxation is a technique in which a person alternately tenses and relaxes each muscle group one at a time from the foot to the head. *Relaxation response* is a similar technique except that all of the muscles are relaxed at once. In *autogenic training*, an individual concentrates on the sensations of warmth and heaviness to relax muscles. *Meditation* focuses on both muscular and mental relaxation to produce a feeling of peace and rest. *Biofeedback* uses instruments to measure the body's immediate state of tension. By watching monitors or listening to signals while practicing relaxation techniques, a person can learn to control involuntary functions such as heart rate and blood pressure.

Relaxation training must be learned and practiced in order to be useful. Self-help books are available on progressive relaxation, meditation, and relaxation response. Local hospitals and schools sometimes offer courses in these methods as well. Biofeedback can be learned only at special clinics with the use of machinery and trained technicians who teach the technique. (See also STRESS-MANAGEMENT TECHNIQUES.)

Responsibility

Responsibility is being accountable for your decisions and actions. People who act responsibly are reliable and trustworthy. They accept the consequences of their actions, and they strive to act in ways that are beneficial to themselves and to other people.

Responsibility. *Responsible parents give their children the love, care, time, and attention that the children need.*

Responsibility affects all aspects of life, including personal health and RELATIONSHIPS with family, friends, and coworkers. People have social responsibilities, moral responsibilities, and legal responsibilities. Taking responsibility for your actions within these broad categories is a sign of emotional and mental maturity.

Learning to be responsible is a process that begins in childhood when parents allow a child to make small, independent decisions, such as choosing what to wear to school. It grows from that point until a person takes full responsibility for his or her life in adulthood.

HEALTHY CHOICES

In order to be responsible members of society, people must first take responsibility for their own lives and behavior. This means adopting a healthful lifestyle that includes good nutrition, adequate exercise, and time for family and friends. Managing your own health enables you to help others more effectively. Responsible people help and care for family members. They can be relied on to fulfil commitments—at school, at work, and in their social lives. Responsible people care enough about the society in which they live to become active and knowledgeable participants.

Role Model

Parents as Role Models. *Parents are a child's first role models and can teach many positive attitudes.*

A role model is someone a person admires and wants to be like. Role models are important influences in teaching behavior, ATTITUDES, and VALUES. Among the most important role models for children and teenagers are parents, older siblings, peers, and, during school years, teachers, counselors, coaches, and students in higher grades. From role models, children learn all kinds of social skills and behavior, both positive and negative.

Psychologists believe that children learn how to act in particular situations by observing and imitating the behavior of other people—*models*—in a process called *observational learning.* The many types of behavior learned through observation include particular skills such as how to shave and drive a car, behavioral responses such as aggressiveness, and attitudes such as prejudice. People are generally more likely to repeat behavior modeled after someone held in high esteem, such as role models.

Parents are a child's first role models, and they teach a great deal through example. A parent who demonstrates healthy behaviors can help the child develop similar behaviors. A parent who is a poor role model, such as a person with an antisocial personality, may teach the child antisocial behavior. The imitation of parental role models is not inevitable, however. The child may see the parent's behavior as negative—an example of what not to do—and may find other role models within the family, school, or neighborhood.

Research has shown that children are more likely to imitate the behavior of a model of the same sex. For example, a girl may observe her mother's successful career in business and her caring attitude toward young children and pattern her behavior after her mother's. (See also ADULT IDENTITY; DEVELOPMENTAL PSYCHOLOGY; FAMILY; HEREDITY AND ENVIRONMENT; SELF-IMAGE; SOCIAL SKILLS.)

SADNESS

see EMOTION

SCHIZOPHRENIA

Schizophrenia is a serious mental disorder characterized by disturbances in behavior, emotions, speech, thoughts, and perception. A person who has this psychotic disorder loses contact with reality and is unable to function normally. Symptoms usually start in adolescence or young adulthood and affect men and women about equally. Schizophrenia currently affects about 1.5 million Americans. It is the most common mental disorder requiring hospitalization in the United States.

The term *schizophrenia* means "split mind," indicating the person's fragmented ways of thinking. The disease should not be confused with MULTIPLE PERSONALITY disorder.

Symptoms People with schizophrenia commonly have *delusions,* which are false ideas that do not correspond to reality. People who have delusions of persecution, for example, falsely believe that someone is out to get them. Those with schizophrenia also suffer from HALLUCINATIONS, which are images, sounds, or smells that do not exist. Their hallucinations are most commonly auditory, in which "voices" tell them how to act or what to do. Visual distortions also occur.

People who have schizophrenia cannot organize their thoughts logically, and they often make no sense when they speak. Some people speak in a jumble of unrelated words called a word salad or make up entirely new words called *neologisms* that have no meaning to anyone else. They may also laugh or cry for no apparent reason. A few people with schizophrenia become aggressive and dangerous, but most are passive and withdrawn and present no threat to others.

Causes The exact cause of schizophrenia is unknown, but inheritance appears to play a role. Family members of people with schizophrenia have a greater chance of developing the illness than do those in the general population. The closer the relationship, the greater the chance.

In addition, physical abnormalities and chemical imbalances have been observed in the brains of those who have schizophrenia. It is not known, however, whether these physical symptoms are a cause or a byproduct of the disease. Environmental factors, including stressful experiences such as serious physical illness and abuse or neglect during childhood, are thought to have some effect on the development of the disease.

Treatment Treatment for schizophrenia consists of *antipsychotic drugs* to reduce the symptoms, combined with PSYCHOTHERAPY to help the person understand and control the disorder. With adequate treatment and support, about one fourth of those affected are able to recover fully and resume a normal life. Most of the rest can recover to some extent, but one out of four needs long-term institutionalization. (See also DRUG THERAPY; PARANOIA; PSYCHOSIS.)

Self-Actualization

Self-actualization is the drive people have to develop their talents and fulfill their potential. It is a key feature of a theory of MOTIVATION developed by American psychologist Abraham Maslow. Maslow explained human motivation in terms of the drive to fulfill one's needs. He believed that human needs fall into three categories: fundamental (food, shelter, and safety); psychological (acceptance, love, and friendship); and self-actualization, which can be realized only when other needs are satisfied.

The Humanistic View Maslow was one of the leaders of the humanistic approach to the study of personality. The approach was developed as an alternative to psychoanalytic and behavioral theories of personality, which were based on studies of disturbed or unhappy individuals. Maslow, however, focused on creative and successful people in an effort to determine what personality traits enabled these people to overcome problems and frustrations and to achieve their goals. He found that these highly "self-actualized" people shared certain qualities. They were curious, spontaneous, open-minded, and independent. He also found that self-actualized people tended to understand their own potential, have a realistic view of the world, and be problem-centered rather than self-centered. They accepted themselves and others as unique individuals, focusing on deep, loving relationships with a few people.

Hierarchy of Needs Maslow placed self-actualization at the highest level of a hierarchy of needs (see chart: Maslow's Hierarchy of Needs). However, people must satisfy their basic needs, those in the lower levels of the pyramid, before concerning themselves with higher needs. He believed that all people have the potential to experience love, self-esteem, and self-actualization, but that few actually realize their creative potential because their basic needs are not met. According to Maslow, achieving self-actualization is not a final goal but part of an ongoing process of growth.

Maslow's critics have argued that his theory takes an overly optimistic view of human beings and what motivates them. However, Maslow's emphasis on the positive characteristics of personality has influenced many psychologists to accept personal growth and self-actualization as useful psychological concepts. (See also PSYCHOLOGY; PSYCHOTHERAPY.)

Maslow's Hierarchy of Needs. *Maslow believed that people must satisfy their fundamental and psychological needs before they can focus on self-actualization.*

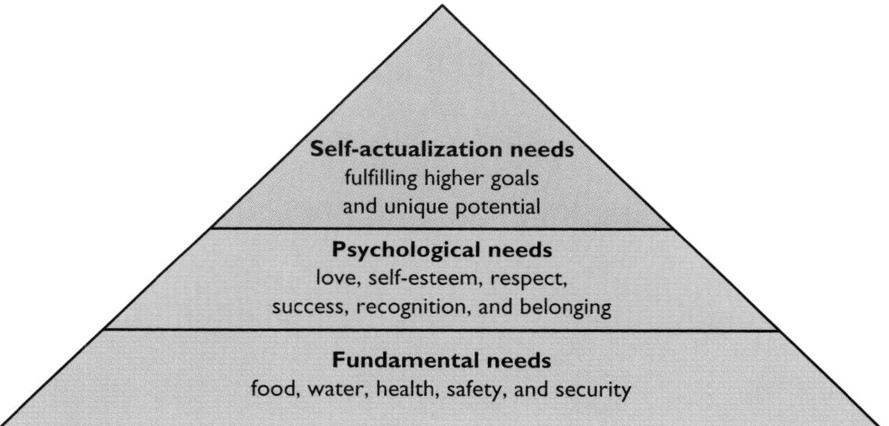

SELF-CONCEPT

see SELF-IMAGE

SELF-EFFICACY

Self-efficacy refers to the confidence people have in their ability to perform new tasks or change behavior. A person with a high degree of self-efficacy feels in control and competent to deal with events, problems, and crises. Self-efficacy is related to SELF-ESTEEM. People with high self-esteem have a positive opinion of themselves and their abilities.

HEALTHY CHOICES

Self-Efficacy and Health A person's level of self-efficacy has a direct bearing on his or her overall health. People with a developed sense of self-efficacy realize that they can do whatever is needed in order to achieve personal goals. This includes decisions about their lifestyles: getting adequate exercise, eating nutritious foods, and avoiding dangerous substances. People with a high degree of self-efficacy have good mental health also. They feel comfortable with themselves and generally face or solve problems rather than overuse DEFENSE MECHANISMS.

Developing Self-Efficacy The characteristics associated with self-efficacy—self-control, ASSERTIVENESS, self-esteem, and a willingness to take intelligent risks—are often thought of as part of maturity. But a feeling of self-efficacy is not limited to adults. It can be found in younger people who have been encouraged by their own experience, or by others, to feel capable of performing well. Parents can play a crucial role in instilling a sense of self-efficacy in their children by allowing them to practice new skills and encouraging them to develop strategies for solving problems.

Experience also plays an important role in developing a sense of self-efficacy. Positive experiences can contribute to feelings of achievement and self-worth. For example, a person who studies hard for a test and does well on it as a result of this effort realizes that he or she has some control over the way things turn out. Negative experiences and a lack of support may also affect a person's sense of self-efficacy. If someone has tried to break a bad habit and failed, he or she often finds it more difficult to try again in the future. In such cases, people can take steps to increase their self-efficacy by focusing on their successes, enlisting the support of others, and moving toward goals in smaller, easier steps that are more likely to have positive results. (See also COPING SKILLS; SELF-ACTUALIZATION; SELF-IMAGE.)

SELF-ESTEEM

Self-esteem is the value each person places on himself or herself. A high level of self-esteem—a sense of personal worth and dignity—contributes to good mental and physical health. Self-esteem is closely related to SELF-IMAGE, the overall perception one has of oneself.

How Self-Esteem Affects Behavior People with *high self-esteem* are more likely to practice good health habits and are less likely to engage in

Childhood and Self-Esteem. *Children whose parents were loving and encouraging are more likely to enjoy high levels of self-esteem in adulthood.*

harmful behaviors, such as excessive drinking, overeating, or drug abuse. A person with high self-esteem will tend to overlook negative responses from other people or view them as rare exceptions. People with *low self-esteem* will usually view positive responses as rare exceptions and negative responses as correct. For example, individuals who have low self-esteem may have difficulty accepting compliments.

Developing and Building Self-Esteem Psychologists believe that the roots of self-esteem can be found in the relationships individuals had with their parents early in childhood. Warm, loving, accepting, and encouraging parents often have children who develop a high level of self-esteem. On the other hand, people who believed their parents thought they were not worthwhile may have grown up believing they are unimportant and incapable. Self-esteem may be affected by other factors as well. Being part of an ethnic or socioeconomic group that is the target of PREJUDICE can also have a negative effect on self-esteem. Having a learning disability or other condition can make it difficult to have high self-esteem.

Adolescents often experience dramatic, but normal, shifts in self-esteem due to natural physical, social, and emotional development. At times, adolescents may feel worthwhile and lovable; at other times, they may feel so unworthy and unlovable that they behave in unpredictable ways in order to receive adult attention and reassurance. Feelings of self-doubt and low self-esteem tend to be more frequent during early adolescence, but they should disappear as the teenager has more occasion to receive positive regard from others. Adolescents who consistently feel unloved, unimportant, or unworthy should share those feelings with a parent or school counselor.

HEALTHY CHOICES

With some effort, everyone can take positive action to improve self-esteem. For example, developing a support group or circle of trusted friends can provide safety and comfort when self-esteem is threatened. Learning to control and take responsibility for personal actions is helpful, as is organizing oneself to make sure tasks are completed successfully and on time. Any achievement, no matter how small, can help a person feel capable, in control, and worthwhile—feelings that contribute to building self-esteem. A person can help others develop high self-esteem by giving sincere feedback and by avoiding unkind criticism or "put-downs." (See also ASSERTIVENESS; PSYCHOTHERAPY; SELF-ACTUALIZATION; SELF-EFFICACY.)

SELF-IMAGE

Self-image is the way a person sees himself or herself. Also called self-concept or identity, self-image encompasses all the thoughts, feelings, and knowledge that you have about yourself. Your self-image affects the way you view the world and your place in it.

Self-image is closely related to SELF-ESTEEM, the value you place on yourself. A person with a realistic self-image tends to set achievable goals; success in attaining these goals helps foster a high level of self-esteem. A self-image that is out of touch with reality, however, can lead

Self-Image. *The feedback received from others contributes to the development of a person's self-image.*

to serious problems. A person with an unrealistic self-image may set goals that are impossibly high, leading to failure, or may set goals that are much too low, resulting in underachievement. Either situation can erode a person's self-confidence and lead to a negative self-image and low self-esteem.

How Self-Image Develops Self-image develops throughout life as people think about themselves and evaluate other people's opinions of them. Self-image is especially influenced by feedback received from parents and teachers in childhood and from peers in adolescence and adulthood. Self-image also develops as people judge their own strengths and weaknesses and evaluate how well they have lived up to their beliefs and values. These processes of self-evaluation generally intensify in adolescence.

From the moment of birth, people classify an individual according to whether he or she is male or female. This *gender identity* becomes a basic element of self-image. Throughout childhood, there is subtle encouragement from parents, teachers, and others to develop qualities and behaviors that are "masculine" or "feminine," that is, behaviors seen as appropriate for boys or girls. These behaviors, called gender roles, influence gender identity and self-image.

Self-Image and Adolescence The self-image developed during childhood undergoes major changes during adolescence. At this stage in their lives, people develop new and more intense friendships, explore new ideas, and become conscious of emerging sexual feelings. In addition, physical growth, social uncertainty, and a strong desire for peer acceptance cause many adolescents to be confused about how they see themselves and their place in the world.

During adolescence the opinions of peers exert a strong influence, but parents' attitudes continue to be important. A teenager may develop a "looking-glass self," which means he or she tends to reflect the opinions of others rather than form his or her own opinions. Reflecting the ideas and values of others may lead some teenagers to lose track of what they believe to be right for them. They may experience an *identity crisis.* A crisis can lead to low self-esteem, or it can help strengthen an individual's sense of self by forcing the individual to define his or her identity.

HEALTHY CHOICES

Self-image becomes more stable and realistic when people consider the opinions of others in light of their experiences, accomplishments, and values. Teenagers with an awareness of their own abilities and the self-confidence to use them are more likely to make a successful transition to adulthood. (See also ROLE MODEL; SELF-ACTUALIZATION; SELF-EFFICACY; GENDER IDENTITY, 6.)

SENILITY

Senility is a general term for the loss of mental function due to old age. It is characterized by a loss of memory, intellectual ability, and awareness of time and place. When symptoms are severe and include changes in personality and behavior, the condition is referred to as *senile dementia.*

Senility is not an inevitable result of aging; only about 20 percent of those older than age 80 have symptoms. In most cases, the symptoms of senility are caused by ORGANIC BRAIN DISORDERS, including Alzheimer's disease and stroke. In some cases, the symptoms are caused by emotional problems such as DEPRESSION, loneliness, and ANXIETY. Senility symptoms may also be caused by drug interactions, which may occur if multiple drugs are prescribed by several physicians who are not aware of all the medications being taken, or by medications taken in inappropriate doses. (See also ALZHEIMER'S DISEASE, 3; DEMENTIA, 3; STROKE, 3.)

RISK FACTORS

SHYNESS

Shyness is a fairly common PERSONALITY trait that causes people to be self-conscious and uncomfortable in social situations. The awkwardness, embarrassment, and ANXIETY that shy people feel at such times occurs because they are overly concerned about what others think of them. Although shy people may want close RELATIONSHIPS, their feelings often hold them back.

Several attempts have been made to explain what causes shyness. According to one theory, shyness develops when people are constantly criticized while they are growing up. Another theory suggests that shyness is largely inherited.

People who are shy only under certain circumstances have *situational shyness*. For example, some people feel shy only when they meet strangers or when they are the focus of attention in large groups. People who are shy in almost all social situations have *chronic shyness*. People with situational shyness can work on overcoming it by being aware of circumstances that trigger their shyness. People with situational or chronic shyness may be helped by taking ASSERTIVENESS training classes. (See also SOCIAL SKILLS.)

Shyness. *Shyness is a distressing trait because it creates barriers to forming close relationships with others.*

SIBLING RIVALRY

Sibling rivalry is competition and jealousy between brothers and sisters in a FAMILY. It is one of parents' most common concerns about their children. Although the cause of frequent quarreling, this rivalry is normal behavior. Even brothers and sisters who argue a great deal tend to play happily together most of the time. Most siblings show concern and support for one another. Sibling rivalry can last from the preschool years, through childhood, and beyond. There is a positive side to sibling rivalry. The interaction helps children learn about themselves and about the feelings and motives of others. It may also allow siblings to establish their individual identities within the family.

Sibling Rivalry. *Sibling rivalry can seem very intense during a competitive sport or game. Severe cases may require family counseling.*

Why Rivalry Occurs Rivalry occurs for many reasons. Siblings are competing for a limited amount of parental time and attention. Brothers and sisters have no choice but to live together in intimate circumstances. Often, siblings have very different personalities; they quickly learn exactly what irritates a brother or sister. Sibling rivalry seems especially intense when the firstborn child must adjust to the arrival of a baby brother or sister. Sibling rivalry may also be intense when children of different parents are merged into a new family unit after a second marriage.

HEALTHY CHOICES

Dealing with Sibling Rivalry If siblings are intensely competitive, they can talk to each other about their feelings. Like any two people in a relationship, siblings can improve their relationship through honest communication, trustworthy, predictable behavior, and respect for the other's privacy and feelings.

Sleep Problems

Almost everyone experiences a disturbance in normal sleeping patterns from time to time. These disturbances become a problem when they are chronic and interfere with a person's ability to function well. Sometimes sleep disorders have physical causes, which can be treated with medication or surgery. They may also be the result of a serious mental health problem, which can be treated with psychotherapy and medication. In many cases, however, sleep problems are caused by a temporary emotional upset or a change in routine.

Insomnia, the inability to fall asleep or stay asleep, is the most common sleep disorder. It may have a physical cause, such as illness or the overuse of caffeine, or it may be a symptom of a serious mental health problem. In many cases, insomnia stems from the tension, excitement, worry, or minor depression brought on by an unsolved problem or an upsetting situation. It can also be caused by a lifestyle that does not allow for a regular sleep pattern.

RISK FACTORS ▶▶▶▶▶▶

When faced with a period of sleeplessness, some people reach for sleeping pills or alcohol to help them get to sleep, but these drugs cause additional problems. Drugs and alcohol work temporarily, but they disturb the quality of sleep. Long-term use can lead to drug dependence or alcoholism. Insomnia caused by minor emotional or physical problems can be relieved by getting some exercise during the day, but not right before bedtime. Taking a warm bath and drinking warm milk or decaffeinated tea before bedtime are also helpful. People who have trouble sleeping should follow a regular schedule of going to bed and getting up and should avoid taking naps during the day. Breathing deeply and practicing systematic relaxation of each muscle group while lying in bed may help bring on sleep as well. Sometimes even counting sheep works by helping the brain relax.

Insomnia. *When troubled by insomnia, some people find such practices as drinking warm milk or taking a warm bath before bedtime helpful.*

For some people, the problem is sleeping too much or being chronically sleepy. This condition may be caused by a physical illness, medication used to treat an illness, or emotional problems. Treatment of the underlying cause may relieve the tendency toward excessive sleep or sleepiness.

Nightmares and Sleepwalking Nightmares, night terrors, and sleepwalking are three sleep problems that occur primarily among children but may also affect adults. Most children outgrow these conditions; adults may require treatment if the problem interferes with the ability to get sufficient rest. *Nightmares* are frightening or unpleasant DREAMS. They are very common in 5- or 6-year-old children. They may be associated with worry in a child, but they are much more likely to be brought on by emotional upset in adults.

In *night terrors,* a person awakens partially from a deep sleep in a state of panic or fright. The feeling of panic is accompanied by an increase in heart and breathing rate. In the morning, the person usually cannot recall the incident. There is no known reason for night terrors in children, but in adults an ANXIETY DISORDER is often the cause.

Night terrors may be accompanied by *sleepwalking,* in which a person moves around in bed or leaves the bed and walks around in a sound sleep. Sleepwalkers need to be protected from injuring themselves. Children may sleepwalk when they are worried about something. In adults, continued sleepwalking may be a sign of an illness such as epilepsy or of ANXIETY or STRESS. Treatment of the underlying disorder can relieve sleep problems caused by anxiety or emotional trauma. (See also RELAXATION TRAINING; STRESS-MANAGEMENT TECHNIQUES; SLEEP, **1**; SLEEP DISORDERS; **3**.)

SOCIAL SKILLS

Social skills are the personal qualities and abilities that enable a person to get along with others and to form and maintain satisfying RELATIONSHIPS. As children grow to adulthood, they learn certain "rules" of social behavior from their families, friends, and teachers or by interacting with social groups like clubs and religious organizations. Many of these rules, such as those relating to manners and courtesy, incorporate valuable guidelines for social interaction.

Many different kinds of skills help people get along with others. One of the most basic and important social skills is the ability to communicate, that is, to talk to and listen to others. ASSERTIVENESS is a social skill that allows for the expression of needs and complaints in a forceful and nonthreatening manner. Being able to convey feelings and needs to others, especially in times of crisis and STRESS, is another important social skill. Equally valuable is showing an interest in and a respect for the thoughts and feelings of others. At the same time, however, it is necessary to respect a person's right to privacy. Other qualities include honoring commitments and displaying tolerance toward different people or groups.

Empathy. *When you empathize with someone, you show understanding of what that person is thinking or feeling.*

Some psychologists attribute certain cases of interpersonal difficulties such as SHYNESS to a social skills deficit. A social skills training course may be recommended to help a person learn and practice such skills as starting a conversation, making a complaint, or asking for permission. Social skills training groups are often run by school psychologists. (See also COMMUNICATION; CONFLICT RESOLUTION; FRIENDSHIP.)

SOCIOPATH

see ANTISOCIAL PERSONALITY

STRESS

Stress is the body's response to any physical or mental demand made on it. Whatever prompts a stress response is called a *stressor.* Stress can be divided into two types. *Eustress* is a positive and desirable stress response, such as the stress produced by moderate exercise or a happy event. Stressors such as family problems or the death or loss of a loved one would produce *distress*, stress that affects you negatively. Distress can damage your physical health and psychological well-being.

Many researchers believe that the effects of stress have less to do with the stressor itself than with how an individual reacts to the stressor.

The effects of stress on the individual depend on many factors. These include the type of stressor, its intensity and duration, and the individual's response to the stressor. Some people adapt well to stress and even find it makes their lives more interesting; others adapt poorly. Many researchers believe that the effects of stress have less to do with the stressor itself than with how an individual reacts to the stressor.

Types of Stressors Major life changes that require a person to adapt to new circumstances often cause stress. A Social Readjustment Rating Scale, compiled in 1967 by Thomas Holmes and Richard Rahe, ranks the stress level of various life events. Highest on the list is death of a spouse (100 life change units, or LCUs); a minor violation of the law is lowest with 11 LCUs. A score of over 300 LCUs indicates a high level of stress; this high a score seems to be associated with certain physical and psychological problems.

Since this scale was established, psychologists like Richard Lazarus have suggested that day-to-day "hassles" may be even more significant stressors. Everyday hassles are the repetitive, routine problems of life. They include physical stressors such as temperature extremes, loud noise, glaring lights, illness, and lack of sleep. Other hassle stressors are emotional (unresolved personal conflict or arguments with friends or family); intellectual (difficult courses, exams); social (demands from family or friends); occupational (a demanding job, a repetitive job, tight deadlines); and spiritual (conflicts in personal or moral beliefs).

The Physiology of Stress When a person experiences a stressful situation, the body reacts with a predictable physiological response. Hans Selye, a leading stress researcher, has described a three-stage stress reaction called the *general adaptation syndrome* (GAS).

- First is the *alarm stage*, during which the AUTONOMIC NERVOUS SYSTEM works with the *endocrine system* to prepare the body for action. Glands in the body secrete chemicals called hormones that cause blood sugar levels to increase, blood pressure and heart rate to rise, and breathing to accelerate.
- The second stage is *resistance*, during which the body is working to combat the stressor. Hormone levels remain high in this stage.
- If the stressor remains, the third stage, *exhaustion*, sets in as the body loses its ability to keep producing the hormones needed to sustain energy. The body's ability to fight stress declines during this period. (See also ENDOCRINE SYSTEM, **1**.)

When a stressor lasts a short time, and when a person is able to relax afterward, blood pressure and hormone levels quickly return to normal. For example, speaking in public may cause the amount of certain chemicals in the blood to rise sharply, but once the person has given the speech and relaxed, the levels will soon return to normal. When stress continues to build up without relief, however, muscle tension, blood pressure, and heart rate remain high for several days or even longer, and the normal functioning of the body may be affected.

Types of Stressors. *Many psychologists are now realizing the importance of everyday "hassles" that may lead to stress-related illnesses over time. Of course, most people are already aware of the disturbing effects on an individual of events such as the death of a loved one.*

The Link Between Stress and Disease Long periods of unrelieved stress seem to reduce the body's ability to fight disease. When hormones increase blood sugar levels to meet energy demands (during the alarm and resistance phase of the general adaptation syndrome), they also decrease the number of certain white blood cells that help fight invading microorganisms. As a result, the immune system is suppressed, making a person more vulnerable to infections. (See also IMMUNE SYSTEM, 1.)

There is evidence of a link between high levels of stress and diseases such as *hypertension* (high blood pressure) and *heart disease.* Evidence suggests that stress may contribute to other disorders as well, including diabetes, cancer, and kidney disorders. (See also PSYCHOSOMATIC DISORDERS; HEART DISEASE, 3; HYPERTENSION, 3.)

Some psychologists believe that your personality influences how you respond to stressors, and this in turn influences your susceptibility to stress-related disease. They say that some people are by nature more susceptible to the damaging effects of stress and are therefore at greater risk of illness. According to this theory, people with *Type A personalities* tend to behave competitively, speak rapidly, show hostility and anger, and struggle constantly to achieve goals in the shortest possible time. People with *Type B personalities* are more calm, serene, and relaxed. When individuals with Type A personalities are confronted with stressors, they may react by secreting higher levels of hormones, which may increase the risk of heart disease and other illness.

HEALTHY CHOICES

Coping with Stress Learning to deal with stress in the modern world is a challenge. A good first step is to develop a lifestyle that focuses on sound physical and MENTAL HEALTH. This makes the body more resistant to the effects of prolonged stress. Such a lifestyle includes good nutrition, regular exercise, and regular relaxation as well as a mental outlook that is positive and adaptable.

Exercise and relaxation are important for another reason. Exercise helps use up the chemicals produced in the stress response. It gives the body relief from their damaging effects. Deliberate relaxation through RELAXATION TRAINING can also provide relief.

Finally, analyzing and dealing with troubling stressors are important factors in handling stress. If stress can be resolved quickly, its damage to the body will be minimal. If a period of stress is prolonged and becomes too difficult to handle, however, then help is needed. Discussing the situation with a parent, friend, teacher, or counselor can help you see the stressors you are facing more clearly. It may enable you to realize that a stressor is less threatening than you thought and help you draw up plans to deal with other stressors. Planning and organization can be a great help in avoiding or managing stress. (See also COPING SKILLS; STRESS-MANAGEMENT TECHNIQUES.)

STRESS-MANAGEMENT TECHNIQUES

Stress-management techniques are constructive ways of preventing and coping with STRESS. Reducing stress can have a positive effect on the quality of life. Reducing stress may also be important to physical health because high levels of stress are linked to such health problems as hypertension, heart disease, and other disorders.

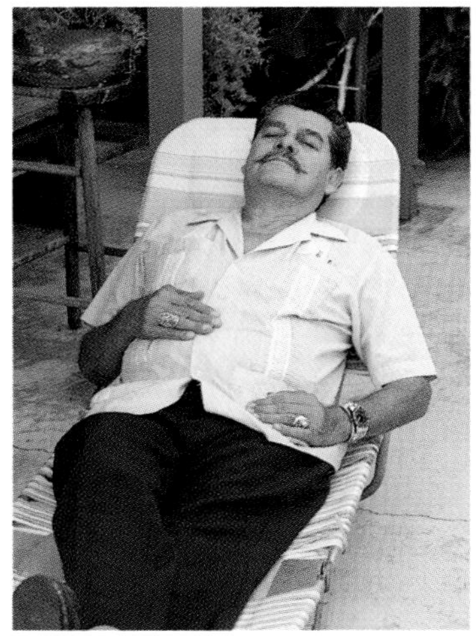

Learning to Relax. *A number of books are available that outline progressive relaxation techniques. These techniques can be used by nearly anyone for managing stress.*

Stress is a normal part of life, and one key to good health is learning to manage stress effectively. Strategies for managing stress include certain psychological techniques, exercise, and relaxation techniques. In addition, positive lifestyle changes can help relieve stress as well as make people more resistant to the negative effects of stress.

Psychological Techniques Developing a positive mental outlook can help you cope with stress. Try to look at stressful situations as problems to be solved. Whenever possible, solve the problems quickly to avoid additional worry about the outcome. Recognize that stress is an inevitable part of life and that it can often have beneficial results. For example, getting a leading role in the school's musical production can result in a very hectic schedule as you try to balance the demands of school work, rehearsals, and responsibilities at home. But the new activity will also bring many rewards. Focusing on the positive aspects of this stressful situation will help manage the stress involved. Good time-management practices will also help.

Exercise You may have experienced the sense of physical relaxation that occurs after vigorous exercise such as jogging and cycling. This is evidence of how exercise helps the body deal with the effects of stress. When the body experiences stress, it boosts the levels of certain hormones in the bloodstream and increases muscle tension. Exercise helps use up these hormones and reduce muscle tension. Exercise also increases strength, flexibility, and endurance, making the body better equipped to handle stress that occurs in the future. *Aerobic exercise*—such as running, swimming, cycling, and aerobic dance—is particularly effective in reducing the effects of stress. (See also AEROBIC EXERCISE, 4.)

HEALTHY CHOICES

Relaxation Practicing one of the many popular relaxation techniques is another way to manage stress. These techniques include progressive relaxation, biofeedback, meditation, and autogenic training.

Progressive relaxation is perhaps the easiest technique to learn. To relax, a person alternately tenses and relaxes groups of muscles, working slowly and in order (from the feet to the head, for instance) until the whole body is relaxed. A quiet room, a comfortable mat or chair, and possibly some soothing background music can enhance relaxation. By practicing this technique twice a day for 15 minutes per session, a person should be able to relax the entire body in a short time. BIOFEEDBACK can help people develop control over body processes such as blood pressure and heartbeat. A machine records these processes electronically, allowing the individual to find out which relaxation techniques or states of mind result in a more relaxed body, as indicated by changes in these processes. *Meditation,* which includes a number of different techniques, helps achieve a relaxed mind and body by combining physical relaxation with concentration on an image or thought to clear and calm the mind. *Autogenic training* focuses the mind on relaxing sensations, such as heaviness or warmth, to bring about mental and physical relaxation.

Positive Changes Sometimes people can make changes in habits, behaviors, and thoughts that are contributing to their own stress. For example, students often feel a great deal of stress before tests, papers, or projects, especially if they have put off preparing or studying for them until the last minute. They may find it helpful to establish priorities in their schedule, planning time for study assignments before doing other activities. Other situations can be helped by changing or eliminating the source of stress. Some adolescents, for example, find parental and teacher expectations to be a source of stress. They may be able to deal better with these expectations by talking to parents and teachers about personal goals and working out realistic learning plans. If stress of any type becomes unmanageable, it is important to seek help by discussing the situation with a friend, relative, teacher, or counselor.

In cases of severe stress or emotional trauma, consult a mental health professional. Crisis counseling, a support group, or group or individual therapy may be necessary in order to manage the effects of the stressful experience. (See also COPING SKILLS; RELAXATION TRAINING.)

SUICIDE

Suicide is the taking of one's own life. Most people who commit suicide suffer from severe DEPRESSION, which is often characterized by feelings of despair, loneliness, and hopelessness. Suicide is also linked to STRESS. Research has shown that suicides among young people are often triggered by stressful events such as unwanted pregnancies, the breakup of relationships, struggles about sexual identity, and problems at home or in school.

Groups at Risk The risk of suicide is greater among certain age-groups and professions. Teenagers, young adults, and the elderly are more likely than are other age-groups to commit suicide. In fact, among teenagers and young adults, suicide attempts have increased

Suicide-Prevention Hot Line. *Hot lines for crisis intervention are listed in the front of most phone books. These community services provide valuable help to people who feel unable to cope with their problems.*

dramatically in recent years, and it is now one of the leading causes of death for those age-groups. Suicide among the elderly sometimes takes the form of refusing food or medical treatment. Certain professions, such as doctors, dentists, and lawyers, have a higher risk of suicide. An increased rate of suicide is also noted among people with substance-abuse problems.

Warning Signs Recognizing the warning signs of a potential suicide can help prevent it. Severe depression is one warning sign of the possibility of a suicide attempt. People who are severely depressed often withdraw from family and friends. Extreme mood swings are another sign. A person whose mood changes dramatically from one day to the next may be struggling with the conflicting desires to live and die. A third warning sign is the giving away of possessions—an indication that the person may be "tidying up" his or her affairs. Talk of suicide is also a warning sign. Suicidal people often mention thoughts of suicide before they act. In addition, a highly stressful event, such as breaking up with a boyfriend or girlfriend or failing several classes, should be viewed as signaling the potential for suicide, especially in those who have already shown signs of depression.

How to Help Talk of suicide and suicidal behavior are often attempts to get help. A person who reveals thoughts of suicide should be encouraged to talk about it with a trained counselor who can assess suicide potential. Communicating suicidal thoughts can help people overcome their self-destructive impulses. In addition, knowing that someone cares and will listen can be a great comfort. Individuals trained in CRISIS INTERVENTION, such as professional counselors and community hot line operators, are further sources of help for suicidal people. A national suicide hot line (1-800-621-4000) is also available. (See also PSYCHOTHERAPY.)

VALUES

Values are the abstract ideas individuals hold about what is right and wrong and what is desirable and objectionable. Values can be influenced by religious or philosophical beliefs, cultural background, family ethics, peer group pressure, and personal experience. Although values do not explicitly tell people how to behave, these ideas help people develop rules, or *norms*, that govern behavior. Values help individuals evaluate their self-worth and the worth of other people, objects, and events; as a result, they influence everyday behavior and the choices individuals make throughout their lives.

Although values may vary from culture to culture, individuals generally share values with other people in their society. In fact, values held in common by a society can help knit a group of people together and move individuals to make sacrifices to preserve their society's values. In turn, values can cause conflict when one person's values are at odds with those of another. For instance, a lawmaker who values national security may vote to spend money on defense, whereas a legislator who values

Values. *Adolescents often express their emerging values by becoming intensely involved in an issue they feel is important.*

social equality may want the money spent on welfare programs to help the underprivileged.

Even within an individual, values can cause conflict. A person may value both financial security and humanitarianism and may thus be torn between taking a high-paying corporate job and a low-paying position as a community action coordinator. Resolution of such conflicts often serves to clarify values and help people make responsible decisions in the future.

Value Development Young children do not have highly developed values. Although they think that specific behaviors are either right or wrong, they do not consider the abstract principles that determine how an action is judged. During adolescence, a new focus on values emerges as young people begin to evaluate the values they have been taught and to consider alternative values. This preoccupation with values during adolescence, a time of focus on self, sometimes leads teenagers to believe that their views are unquestionably right and that the beliefs of parents or other adults are misplaced, hypocritical, or shallow. This somewhat extreme point of view declines as teenagers have an opportunity to discuss values with others and to see things from different points of view.

Changing Values Just as an individual's values may change as the person grows, so the values of a society may change. Such changes may be set off when conditions within the society change. For instance, throughout World War II, the values of freedom and nationalism assumed a great deal more importance in the United States than did the values of material comfort and financial security as people came together to fight the war. Changes in a society's values can also occur when a group within the society is able to convince the majority that they have been wrong. For instance, protests by African-Americans, women, and other groups that have been discriminated against in the United States have brought about a greater insistence on the value of equality. (See also ATTITUDES; FAMILY; RESPONSIBILITY.)

SUPPLEMENTARY SOURCES

Bloom, Floyd E., and Arlyne Lazerson. 1988. *Brain, mind, and behavior.* New York: W. H. Freeman.

Bruno, Frank J. 1989. *The family mental health encyclopedia.* New York: Wiley.

Carskadon, Mary A., ed. 1993. *Encyclopedia of sleep and dreaming.* New York: Macmillan.

DiCanio, Margaret. 1989. *The encyclopedia of marriage, divorce, and the family.* New York: Facts On File.

Dinner, Sherry H. 1989. *Nothing to be ashamed of: Growing up with mental illness in your family.* New York: Lothrop, Lee & Shepard.

Friedland, Bruce. 1988. *Emotions and thoughts.* New York: Chelsea House.

Friedland, Bruce. 1991. *Personality disorders.* New York: Chelsea House.

Gilbert, Sara. 1982. *What happens in therapy.* New York: Lothrop, Lee & Shepard.

Hanson, Peter G. 1986. *The joy of stress.* New York: Andrews, McMeel & Parker.

Kaplan, L. S. 1990. *Coping with peer pressure.* New York: Rosen Publishing Group.

Leder, Jane M. 1987. *Dead serious: A book for teenagers about teenage suicide.* New York: Atheneum.

Lee, Essie E., and Richard Wortman. 1986. *Down is not out: Teenagers and depression.* New York: Julian Messner.

Matthews, John R. 1991. *Eating disorders.* New York: Facts On File.

Powell, Barbara. 1987. *Good relationships are good medicine.* Emmaus, Pa.: Rodale Press.

Rice, Phillip L. 1987. *Stress and health.* Monterey, Calif.: Brooks/Cole Publishing.

Sherman, Roberta T., and Ron Thompson. 1990. *Bulimia: A guide for family and friends.* Lexington, Mass.: Lexington Books.

Squire, Larry R., ed. 1992. *Encyclopedia of learning and memory.* New York: Macmillan.

University of California, Berkeley. 1991. *The wellness encyclopedia.* Boston: Houghton Mifflin.

ORGANIZATIONS

Alzheimer's Association
919 North Michigan Avenue
Chicago, IL 60611
(800) 272-3900

American Anorexia/Bulimia Association
418 East 76th Street
New York, NY 10021
(212) 734-1114

American Association for Marriage and Family Therapy
1100 17th Street, NW
10th Floor
Washington, DC 20036
(202) 452-0109

American Institute of Child Health and Human Development
9000 Rockville Pike
Bethesda, MD 20892
(301) 496-4000

American Institute of Stress
124 Park Avenue
Yonkers, NY 10703
(914) 963-1200

American Psychiatric Association
1400 K Street, NW
Washington, DC 20005
(202) 682-6000

American Psychological Association
1200 17th Street, NW
Washington, DC 20036
(202) 336-5500

Anxiety Disorders Association of America
6000 Executive Boulevard
Suite 513
Rockville, MD 20852
(301) 231-9350

Association for Applied Psychophysiology and Biofeedback
10200 West 44th Avenue
Wheat Ridge, CO 80033
(303) 422-8436

Association for Retarded Citizens
The (ARC)
500 East Border Street
Suite 300
Arlington, TX 76010
(817) 261-6003

Family Service America
11700 West Lake Park Drive
Milwaukee, WI 53224
(414) 359-1040

Institute for Mental Health Initiatives
4545 42nd Street, NW
Suite 311
Washington, DC 20016
(202) 364-7111

National Association for Down Syndrome
P.O. Box 4542
Oak Brook, IL 60522
(708) 325-9112

National Institute of Mental Health
Public Inquiries Section
5600 Fishers Lane
Rockville, MD 20857
(301) 443-4515

National Mental Health Association
1021 Prince Street
Alexandria, VA 22314
(703) 684-7722

National Stroke Association
300 East Hampden Avenue
Englewood, CO 80110
(303) 762-9922

Office of Disease Prevention and Health Promotion
National Health Information Center
P.O. Box 1133
Washington, DC 20013
(800) 336-4797

Parents Without Partners
8807 Colesville Road
Silver Spring, MD 20910
(301) 588-9354

President's Committee on Mental Retardation
330 Independence Avenue, SW
Washington, DC 20201
(202) 619-0634

Single Parent Resource Center
141 West 28th Street
Suite 302
New York, NY 10001
(212) 947-0221

Stepfamily Association of America
215 Centennial Mall South
Suite 212
Lincoln, NE 68508
(402) 477-7837

INDEX

Italicized page numbers refer to illustrations or charts.